Making Gravy In Public

JON DAWSON

ISBN: 0615580726
ISBN-13: 978-0615580722

THANKS:

Laura, Emma, Ava, Patrick Holmes, Bryan Hanks, Charlie Kraebel, Janet Carter, Paulette Burroughs, Nancy Saunders, Shana Norris, Correai Moore, Paul Dawson, Paul DeBoy, John Johnson, Jon Hughes, Michael Gagliano, Sue Smith, David Anderson, Wes Brown, Justin Hill, Jane Moon, Cecil Burke, June Cummings.

CONTENTS

EMERGENCY CREWS STORM GOLF COURSE ON FAMILY NIGHT
JUNE 16, 2011

DISCLAIMER: In the following column the term "putt-putt" will be used to describe the practice of hitting a golf ball with a putter on a miniature golf course. The correct term for this activity is "miniature golf," but I've called it "putt-putt" for 38 years, and I refuse to switch horses this late in the race. The term "putt-putt" is not to be confused with "Putt-Putt," which is a registered trademark of Putt-Putt Fun Center. Also, the artist formerly known as "Kathy Lee Gifford" will now be referred to as "Satan."

Last weekend was a weekend of firsts for the Dawson family. For starters, we took our 14-month-old daughter to the beach for the first time. We assumed that she'd give the ocean the ol' hairy eyeball for a while and gradually ease up to it, but she ran towards it like a puppy toward a truck full of fire hydrants. There is nothing like watching your baby squidge her little foot into the wet sand for the first time. She had the same look on her face that I had when I realized the drink machine in The Free Press break room didn't know the difference between a quarter and the buttons from the coats in the lost and found.

The other big news is that I took our 6-year-old daughter on her first putt-putt/bumper-boat expedition. When we arrived at the Golfin' Dolphin that fateful Friday evening, neither of us was aware of the epic journey that lay before us.

The first thing she had to do was choose the color of her putter. Naturally, she gravitated toward the pink, and she was puzzled as to why I didn't want to get a pink one so we'd match. She was then fascinated by the fact that we could keep the pencil provided with the score card. I've spent hours searching for gifts that got half the reaction of that jinky little pencil, but I digress.

After a brief discussion of the rules, we teed off on the first hole. It was a par 3 and I think she had a quintuple bogey. Eventually she realized putt-putt was less about swinging wildly like an airplane without wings, and more about finesse and planning ahead. She went on to make par on many holes, and she even got a birdie on the seventh hole. If you count the sea gull she accidentally winged while swinging her club, then she actually got two birdies.

Father and daughter were both having a good time winding our way through the twists and turns of the course like coffee through a nervous bladder. All of that changed, however, when we came upon a mother/father/son trio that was ahead of us.

I don't mean to get all Bob Ross up in here, but allow me to paint a word picture for you: It was obvious these folks weren't from around here. The dad alone had three separate pouches attached to his belt — a belt that was holding up a pair of shorts. One pouch appeared to house a camera, the second probably a cell phone and the third, by my estimation, had to have been filled with some sort of hallucinogenic mushrooms and/or trail mix.

When we started there was no one even close to us, so by my estimation that had to have been on at least the fifth or sixth hole when we started. Normally I'm the most impatient man on the planet, but the daughter kept me busy with plenty of questions ("What are golf balls made out of?", "Why does Katie Couric have a career?") and there was a pleasant ocean breeze, so I just relaxed and affixed my gaze on the family ahead of us in hopes they'd do something I could write about.

While they were all peculiar, the dad seemed to be the ringleader. On more than one occasion I saw this man spend several minutes clearing the putting surface of teeny-tiny bits of pine straw that Horatio Cane would have overlooked. Also, when the son accidentally knocked the ball out of bounds, instead of allowing a do-over, he pulled out his Blackberry so he could look up the official rules online. According to the rules provided by the National Putt-Putt Association, the son could either take a penalty stroke or be smashed in the head with his own putter by those playing in his group. I admired the son's moxy for taking that shot to the head, but by the looks of him he was already a little slow on the draw anyway.

Between the 12th and 13th holes the mom noticed a nest of newborn kittens under an adjacent bush. Whereas most earthlings would just say something like "how cute" and get on with their lives, these people set up camp. Apparently the dad went to high school with Mutual of Omaha's Jim Fowler, because within minutes a helicopter full of zoologists landed via helicopter on the 18th green. Within minutes the kittens were spayed, neutered, washed and issued insurance policies.

Eventually we made it to the last hole, which as many seasoned putt-putters will know is equipped with a pipe that carries your ball away after it falls into the cup. The Family of Dr. Moreau, however, was new to this concept. The mom was so confused that she assumed she'd knocked her ball off the course and went up to the putt-putt hut to request another ball.

An incredibly patient employee explained that her ball had in fact fallen into the cup and through the miracle of PVC pipe been delivered back to the holding area. Father and son eventually finished their round, which allowed us to do the same.

After putt-putt my daughter and I headed over to the bumper-boat area. I hadn't been in a bumper boat since I was around 10-years-old, and apparently those things are not made for 6-foot men who are on the north side of petite. I got in the boat fine, but my feet had to hang over the edge, which made it look like I was sitting on a giant motorized hemmorhoid pillow.

While we were in the middle of the bumper-boat pool — spinning in a circle at 30 mph — we discovered the boat's water gun feature. The daughter promptly pulled the trigger and unleashed a water stream of tsunami proportions in the general direction of the Moreau Family. Don't worry though; the dad had a full pack of ponchos in his back pocket.

THE DISCOUNT GIGOLO
OCTOBER 23, 2008

When I decided to run for president, I knew the media elite would dig through my past. Thankfully, they haven't found any skeletons in my closet.

As a matter of fact, most of my skeletons are running loose.

One thing those thugs at MSNBC and Fox have dug up, though, is my stint as a professional wrestler. Not much footage of my wrestling career exists, because most of my bouts took place at boat shows and used car lot openings.

Although I'm not proud of my past as a professional wrestler, I did make the most of the experience. My wrestling name was "Andre, The Discount Gigolo;" I would prance to the stage dressed in a tuxedo, handing out coupons for free back rubs to all the ladies in the crowd.

If I won the wrestling match, I would humiliate my opponent by taking his wife out to dinner at the Sizzler.

Every wrestler worth his salt had a great theme song: The Rock had "Can You Smell What the Rock is Cookin'?" and Batista uses "Line in the Sand" by Motorhead.

I was no exception. My theme song evoked the essence of my character. In fact, my theme song is now being used by Subway restaurants in their latest ad campaign.

That's right, "$5 Foot Long" was originally written for my wrestling alter ego, "Andre, The Discount Gigolo." Apparently, Bill O'Reilly and Keith Olbermann were searching YouTube for examples of bias in the media, and one of my appearances at a "Hugs Not Drugs" rally popped up.

The song was so catchy that the heads of both networks convinced Subway to use it in their new campaign.

In 1990, while performing at a benefit for the Flatulence League of Greater Chicago, I was attacked by a fan. A bloated-looking fellow wearing a

"Silent But Deadly" T-shirt snuck up behind me and hit me over the head with a chair. When I came to, I was in the hospital. I was surrounded by all of the people that cared about me: My agent and my accountant.

I was informed that my contract would not be picked up by the World Wrestling Federation. For the next few months, I spent my days eating raw cookie dough, sitting on the edge of the couch and staring at the floor.

After it became impossible to wade through my own drool without wearing galoshes, I pulled myself up by the bootstraps and decided to enter the high-paying world of politics.

Sure, I have no discernible talent, but that hasn't stopped Joe Biden or Sarah Palin from shooting to the top of their profession.

Biden has ripped off other peoples speeches and Palin thinks she can see Putin tying his shoes from her back porch.

When I steal from someone else's speeches, I at least take the time to blackmail the original author first.

The only thing I can see from my back porch is the shiny red "Open" sign at the local ABC store. A little part of me dies every time that light is turned off.

Now, in reference to last week's column, a printing error caused the last line to be cut off. To see the whole column with its super-duper closing line, visit my blog address below.

Keep hope alive.

SHOULD MEN SHOP TOGETHER?
JULY 10, 2008

Last week my friend, Correai Moore, was in town and he met me at work just as I was heading out. He had to head back to Chapel Hill, but had time to hang out for a minute. I had to pick something up at the local book store for my daughter, so he met me there.

To give you a visual, Correai looks kind of like Eddie Murphy, without the money, women or talent.

I'm sort of a cross between Lyle Alzado and Carrot Top.

After we left the book store, we started talking and before we knew it we had kibitzed our way down to JC Penney.

Usually, I'd rather clean the toilets in a Turkish prison than have to go clothes shopping, but there was a massive sale going on, so we checked it out. We discovered the store had winter coats that were normally $60 reduced to $15, jeans 50 percent off; I tell you, we got a little emotional.

Anyway, about 10 minutes later it hit me in the face like a dead carp: we were clothes-shopping ... together.

I froze in the middle of the store like a deer staring at a Peterbilt.....I was frightened, but too scared to move.

After a long silence, I asked Correai if he had he noticed we were clothes shopping. At that moment, a look of concern crossed his face. We immediately started rattling off sports stats and the chronological order of the models that appeared on the cover of Maxim magazine.

Anyway, it gets better.

Correai, like me, isn't awash in cash. He was getting paid the next day, but the sale was ending at the close of business. I told him that I would pay for it with my credit card (I get points for airline tickets), and that he could pay me back later.

6

We go up to the counter, and he throws the clothes on the counter, and I get out the credit card. We both immediately realize that the attractive sales lady thinks we're a couple - not that there's anything wrong with that.

As we left the store, we felt that we had learned something. Was it a lesson in tolerance? No. We learned that we should never speak of this again, unless we need an idea for a column.

Epilogue: The next day, Correai stopped by my house. My wife does alterations and he had some things that needed mending. After he explained to her what repairs he needed, he handed me a pair of the pants purchased the previous day.

"Whenever you go by the mall again, can you return these? They ended up not being a good fit," he said.

Yes, I'm returning pants for another man.

We shopped, we dropped, get used to it!

STRANDED MOTORISTS BREAK INTO
GROCERY STORE, GET MARRIED
JANUARY 29, 2009

Last week's snow storm caused a lot of trouble in Lenoir County. Ditches and medians were littered with vehicles, grocery stores were overrun by people on a quest to stock up on Spam and beer and middle-aged men who thought they were still young busted their butts en masse.

As the day progressed, the storm got worse. I had to prepare for a road trip, so I left the office around 1 p.m. While preparing to leave, Paulette Burroughs asked if I would drive her home, as she was wary of driving her Honda on the ice.

And it came to pass that Paulette and I loaded into my 1993 Chevrolet Suburban and started easing down the road towards La Grange.

The first few minutes of the trip were normal enough; we shared some office gossip, split a tin of Vienna sausages, and washed it down with some warm Fresca. A couple of times Paulette rolled down her window to throw lit cigarettes at pedestrians; it was a good time.

As we turned off of U.S. 70 at Wynn Odom Ford, I lost control of the truck and we slid off the road and down an embankment. When we came to, it was dark and extremely cold. The truck was upside down, while we suspended in mid-air by our seatbelts.

I managed to unhook my seatbelt and got Paulette down as well. We crawled out of the truck to find no businesses open, and no traffic on the road. My cell phone was dead and Paulette had lost hers in a poker game.

We started walking towards town, hoping to find some signs of life. We made it to a grocery store, but it was closed. Paulette pulled out a hairpin and picked the lock. Once inside, Paulette headed straight to the wine section. Before I could open a box of Triscuits, Paulette had downed a bottle of Courvoisier.

It was cold inside the store, so I rounded up several cases of diapers, doused them with lighter fluid, and lit 'em up. Paulette took a roll of duct tape and used several bags of cotton balls to fashion a couple of pillows.

As we dined on a supper of cheese whiz and bananas, the flaming Pampers created quite a romantic mood. The light from the fire danced off Paulette's glasses like a group of Shriner's waiting to get in the bathroom.

We huddled together for warmth, and just like in the movies, a romance blossomed.

In the morning, we awoke to find a visibly shaken stock boy poking us with a broom. After we wiped the sleep dirt from our eyes, we started to notice that seemingly all of La Grange had gathered around our makeshift camp. Folks from all walks of life (from housewives and bankers to wards of the state and Duke fans) all joined as one to try and figure out what was going on.

While the general feeling in the store was that something unholy and filthy had taken place, Paulette and I knew different; we were in love. We immediately made plans to wed in the summer.

If you'd like to buy a gift, we are registered at Big Blue in Kinston.

NYQUIL BEGAT ELVIS
AUGUST 16, 2008

As I'm sure thousands of you read on my blog last weekend, I was at home sick on Friday. I gave it a valiant effort though; I crawled into the office at 7a.m. and started updating www.kinston.com.

About 15-minutes into it, I realized that it was a horrible mistake coming into work. I was so out of my gourd with a fever that I wrote a biting social commentary about chalk poachers in Indonesia, but after roughly 30 www.kinston.com readers called in to complain, I was able to remove the article before either of my bosses saw it.

I called Content Editor Bryan Hanks and offered to buy him a Britney Spears t-shirt if he would allow me to work from home. He was fine with it as long as I threw in a Liberace CD. Fair enough. I went around the office and coughed on everybody's phone and hit the highway.

After fighting the good fight for about six hours I pulled the plug. I'm not a fan of taking alot of medicine, but I was either going to have to install a drip pan to catch the sweat or qwell the fever that was now 101 degrees. I asked my beautiful wife for some Nyquil, and she walked off to the kitchen to get the medicine. She came back wearing a HAZMAT suit, and she dangled the Nyquil over my head with a pool skimmer. She then shut the door and preceded to duct-tape the edges so that nothing I emitted would travel to the rest of the house.

Did I mention that my daughter had this same cold earlier in the week?

My wife then called my cell phone to say she was going to the grocery store. It was now just me and the cold; mono e germo.

Since I take so little medicine and I'm a tea totaler, the Nyquil knocked me right out. After a few hours of precious sleep, I awoke to find Elvis Pressely sitting in my bedroom.

"How's it going, JD?" said Elvis.

"Not too good," I said. "I've got a fever, my throat feels like a I swallowed a porcupine, and my head is about to crack open."

"It ain't going to good for me either," Elvis said. "When I died in 1977, I didn't go straight to heaven. I had to do some time in purgatory for the drug abuse and what-not. I was finally issued a parking pass for heaven when I got word that my daughter had married E.T., and I had to come back down to earth to bust that up."

He then reached into his Wal-Mart greeter's smock and handed me a fried peanut butter and bananna sandwich with bacon. As I ate the sandwich, I could feel my illness subsiding. As I was thanking Elvis for the sandwich, he stood up and said that he had to go.

"Where are you going now?" I asked.

"I'm finally going to heaven," Elvis said. "But St. Peter said I've got to stop in LaGrange to pick up some barbeque for Bo Diddley and Bill Monroe on the way." We both agreed that since they helped invent Rock and Roll, it was the least he could do.

Elvis got in his Cadillac, popped in a Robert Goulet 8-track, and drove into the sunset. After this I went back to bed for a peaceful sleep.

About an hour later, my wife returned from the grocery store. She woke me up and asked why there were half eaten bananas and peanut butter strewn all over the kitchen floor.

"Rock and Roll, baby," I said. "Rock and roll."

LARCENY AT THE FREE PRESS
AUGUST 21, 2008

Working in an office can be a tricky thing. In most offices little tribes form over time.

All of the sports folks tend to gravitate towards each other. The music and or movie geeks usually meet up at the coffee machine, and the anti-social folks ignore everybody together.

Last week the guy that sat at the desk over from me, Phillip, transferred to our Jacksonville office. Although we still see each other occasionally, I'll still miss the stench of Remy Martin and sardines emanating from his side of the office.

One day last week we were lamenting the loss of Phillip, and it was at this time that we decided to rummage through his desk and see if there was anything good left in it.

For the record, I was not the first one in. I won't reveal who it was because this person could probably get me fired.

The first person that went desk digging found a bag of pecans. Phillip always had grapes or pecans at his desk. None of us ever asked for any of his food because he would make us ask his ever-present hand puppet Marcel.

The bag of pecans got passed around like crazy at a Scientology seminar.

We then started to go through the items left on top of his desk. Photographer Janet Sutton took a little penguin that stood on a barrel. I took the wedding announcement for the Moore/Johnson wedding.

The best find of all was Phillip's chair. I now know why Phillip was usually in a good mood: He had a great chair. I'm usually in a foul mood, but if you saw the Pepsi crate they had me sitting on, you'd know why.

I switched the chairs and the gray film that covered my world was replaced by a Technicolor wash that would rival a Starburst commercial. I could smell colors and see smells. What did they do in that office at night?

Sadly, there was no money in his desk. Apparently Phillip and I borrowed the same 60 cents from each other for nearly nine months.

The only other thing we could find were receipts from a bail bondsmen and a few dozen appointment cards from the free clinic.

Phillip, you may be gone, but your personal belongings will be on eBay for at least 10 more days.

INTERVIEW WITH A FAT MAN
NOVEMBER 11, 2008

Since most retailers have started hawking Christmas items already, I thought it would be a good idea to interview Santa Claus. It's a tad early, but my connections tell me it's hard to get him in December.

The Free Press: Santa, thanks for talking to us today.

Santa: Not a problem.

FP: How do you feel about these stores selling Christmas items in October?

Santa: Well, it does take a lot of attention away from the spiritual aspect of the season. Also, my agent has me going to more and more stores each year. It's good to be in demand, but these knees of mine ain't what they used to be. I've had to install a kick stand to be able to hold these increasingly obese children in my lap.

FP: How many elves do you currently employ?

Santa: Well, NAFTA really opened things up as far as labor goes. I used to employ around 80,000 elves. These days I keep a minimal staff of around 100.

FP: Wow, that means over 79,000 elves are out of work, right?

Santa: Well, as I said earlier, folks are eating like crazy now. Most of my former elves now work for Keebler. Apparently, cookies are very popular.

FP: What about the laid off elves that didn't go to work for Keebler?

Santa: The rest of them were hired by Tom Cruise. Apparently, he only hires people that make him feel tall.

FP: What would you say are the most requested toys this season?

Santa: I'd say the "Tickle-Me Elmo Bullet Proof Vest" and the "Monopoly - Government Buyout Edition" are the top two.

FP: Are there any toys that didn't catch on as well as people where expecting?

Santa: The "John McCain Speedo" and the "Joe Biden Hair Transplant Kit" never made it out of the warehouse. The "Sarah Palin 12-month Bikini/Moose Hunting" calendar has been doing quite well though.

FP: Does Rudolph still lead your sleigh every year?

Santa: Rudolph and I are in the midst of litigation right now; I can't really comment on that.

FP: Does this litigation stem from the discovery of the adult film, "Is That Your Nose?"

Santa: All I can say is that before I employed him to pull my sleigh, Rudolph had to make a living. Some Larry Flint-type saw what Rudolph could do with his nose, and he saw dollar signs.

FP: Well if Rudolph the Red Nose Reindeer isn't leading your sleigh, then who is?

Santa: We've got a good guy this year: Sammy the Sinus Infection Reindeer.

FP: How does having a sinus infection help lead a sleigh?

Santa: Before we take off, Sammy drinks the inside of a couple of glow sticks. Every time he sneezes, it looks like a Pink Floyd concert. It's a beautiful thing.

FP: What's the biggest challenge you face as the years start to add up?

Santa: Alarm systems are a real pain in the tuckus. Also, kids have started leaving celery instead of cookies. I realize that I have a weight problem. I'm workin' on it, okay?

FP: Well Santa, I want to thank you for taking the time to talk to us. Any words for the kids?

Santa: I have a list of who's been naughty and who's been nice. As far as I'm concerned, be as naughty as you want; it'll mean less work for me.

IS KINSTON READY FOR AN AMUSEMENT PARK?
JANUARY 06, 2009

Ever the entrepreneur, I've been working with a group of investors from Scandinavia to bring an amusement park to Kinston.

While nothing is set in stone just yet, the preliminary plans are very exciting.

For starters, the rides will be based on themes that folks in Eastern North Carolina can relate to.

One ride we're working on is called Barbecue Mountain. Kids will be able to climb Barbecue Mountain while wearing buns from the day-old bread store to protect their head, elbows, and knees.

Once they reach the top of Barbecue Mountain, the kids will board a giant hushpuppy and ride down Gravy Falls until they splash into Cole Slaw Canyon.

This is not to be confused with Disney's "Mullet Mountain" or Kings Dominion's "Chewing Tobacco Taco Time."

For the young sportsman, we have an attraction called Bowling for Bambi. In this game, a row of deer are lined up at the end of a long alley and kids will try to take out as many deer as possible.

Note: Camouflaged bowling balls are prohibited and parents are responsible for discarding of any unused deer carcasses.

For you Nintendo fiends, we have an attraction called "Mr. Couch Potato Head". On this ride, the longer you play video games, the more swollen and lethargic "Mr. Couch Potato Head" becomes and the more points you accumulate.

The first player in your group to make "Mr. Couch Potato Head" grow to a size that requires firemen to cut a wall out of his house to get him to the hospital will win a coupon for a free angioplasty.

On paper, I know this looks like a crazy idea, but necessity is the mother of invention. The only thing standing between Kinston and its' very own amusement park is capital. Undaunted, I believe the good readers of this paper are willing to contribute their share to get this thing off the ground.

The Free Press has roughly 15,000 subscribers, and I'm asking each one of you for just $1.

That's right, for $1 you can get in on the ground floor of something that is bound to be as successful as the Hard Rock Café Park in South Carolina.

Send your checks to The Free Press, Attn. Jon Dawson, 2103 N. Queen St., Kinston, 28501. The name of the group putting the park together changes from day to day, so for your convenience, you can simply make the checks payable to "cash".

As an investor, you will receive annual progress reports, a monthly newsletter, and a coupon redeemable for free security services from Paulette Burroughs.

Come on Kinston. Are you going to deny your children giant hushpuppies?

LOCAL MAN ATTACKED BY RARE ANIMAL
JANUARY 08, 2009

While not as rare in nature as Bigfoot or the Dodo bird, the Land Mullet is still one of nature's little quirks.

If you read my column on Tuesday, you may remember there was a section that poked a little fun at folks that sport "mullet" haircuts.

This is how Wikipedia describes The Mullet:

"A mullet is a hairstyle that is short in the front, top, and sides, but long in the back, at least to the shoulder blades. As a result it is sometimes jokingly referred to as 'business in the front, party in the back'."

If you need a visual, David Spade sports a mullet in the movie "Joe Dirt".

Last week I was in Goldsboro, and I remembered that my old barber had a shop over there. I hadn't had a haircut in a while, so I popped in.

It was just like old times. I told him, "just thin it out, the length is fine."

As the scissors flew around my head at lightening speed, I started to wonder what would happen if the guy cutting my hair suddenly had a flashback to an early childhood trauma - would he simply fall to the floor, or would he have a fit and lance my jugular?

Anyway, I made it through the melee without a scratch, and I took my freshly cut and still-wet head home.

That night I got out of the shower and dried my hair. A few seconds later, I saw something in the mirror that would scare Darth Vader to death: I had a mullet.

I made it all through the 1980s without a mullet, and now in 2009, I'd been saddled with one.

I tried every maneuver in the book to get rid of it: water, hair gel, bacon grease, but nothing worked.

The next day, I called Otis Scissorhands back to get it fixed, but he was going to be out of town until the following week.

I went to work the next day hoping nobody would notice it. It was going OK until photographer Janet Sutton strolled in.

"You've got a mullet!", she exclaimed, shaking with laughter.

Reporter Justin Schoenberger then piped in: "Yeah, I was wondering if you had that done on purpose."

I can take a good ribbing as much as the next guy, but sometimes people take things too far.

Bryan Hanks, for example, tried to feed it a cracker, which I thought was over the line.

For the rest of the day I flipped up the collar on my shirt, trying to hide the hairy mudflap growing out of my neck. I sort of looked like a cross between Dracula and Billy Ray Cyrus.

With all other options depleted, my long suffering wife got out the scissors and repaired my damaged head. Considering what she had to work with, she did a great job, and I can now show my face in public with minimal disgrace.

Although it was a pain in the neck - literally - I kind of miss the little fella. I saved him in a Ziploc bag and when I get bored, I throw it in the middle of the newsroom and yell, "RAT!", just to see how many folks will knock their coworkers over to get away from the thing.

If you have a mullet, please don't call me, as I've already gotten grief about Tuesday's column.

In lieu of flowers, please send money to the National Mullet Defense Fund, c/o Jon Dawson at the Free Press, 2103 N. Queen St., Kinston, 28501.

FREE PRESS WRITER CONFRONTS CRITICS
FEBRUARY 12, 2009

Over the past few weeks, I've been swimming in e-mails and online comments. Most of the statements have been positive, but there have been a couple of negative ones.

First of all, my boss, Bryan Hanks, was accosted at the Kinston Utilities Department last week by four women who were deeply concerned about what I was writing about him.

According to Bryan, one woman took him by the hand, looked him in the eye and asked why they let me write such horrible things about him. Another woman said that when I wrote a column about quitting, she cried.

On the other end of the spectrum, a woman asked Bryan if I was wearing a wig in my profile picture. Well, of course I am. Who would walk around like that?

The nicest call I've gotten was from a woman that said her son collected all of my columns in a scrapbook. I gotta tell you folks, that one was surprising.

While it's good to talk about the good things people say, there are always a few folks who think I'm the anti-Christ and that I should be sealed in a concrete bunker six miles underground.

These folks routinely visit www.kinston.com and comment on my columns, and they get pretty vicious.

One user that goes by the name "theeguvnor," thinks I'm the worst thing to come down the pike since tuberculosis. Another poster, "sisterdroolcup," believes I'm Satan's daddy.

While criticism is part of living in a free society, these folks really seem to have a Viagra-induced penchant for giving me grief. It's almost as if they enjoy having me to punch around. I'm not sure if any of the other folks here at The Free Press have been introduced to their rapier wit, but these folks really, really, really don't like me at all.

Now I don't like onions, so I don't eat them. Also, I don't like Rush Limbaugh or Keith Olbermann, as I think they're both different sides of the same coin. For that reason, I don't listen to either one of them. I'm sure lots of you folks do like them, and that is your right. God bless America!

While I don't like Limbaugh or Olbermann, I don't spend valuable time sending them hate mail. I've got more important things to do, like clipping coupons or looking for vintage Milli Vanilli memorabilia on eBay.

Last week I finally had enough of this abuse, so with the help of our Internet team, I tracked down the whereabouts of "theeguvnor" and "sisterdroolcup." With their information in hand, I found out where they worked with the intention of showing up at their place of work and telling them what I thought of their work.

My first stop was a bovine insemination center just outside La Grange. The person that goes by the online moniker "theeguvnor" works there in the husbandry division. I walked through the facility until I saw "theeguvnor" up to his elbow in a Holstein.

I took the opportunity to tell him that his technique was all wrong, that he should at least light a candle and that a little Luther Vandross would probably enhance the mood.

I'd planned to visit "sisterdroolcup" at her place of work, but only authorized personnel are allowed in the Lenoir County sewer system.

I have to say it felt good to heckle a heckler. I'm sure that by doing so I've only caused myself more grief and that my mailbox will be full of angry letters, written mainly in crayon and/or mayonnaise, but that's OK.

I can take it.

FREE PRESS ADDS VITAMINS TO INK
FEBRUARY 17, 2009

With the economy in the ditch, businesses are doing whatever they can to retain customers.

Car dealerships are offering zero-percent financing and pizza restaurants are working day and night to find another crevice to cram some cheese into.

I think the final frontier will be designing a pizza delivery box that is made out of cheese; maybe cheese flavored Pepsi? Cheese napkins?

Newspapers are not immune to this type of gonzo ingenuity. We have to compete with the internet (www.Kinston.com), television and the breakfast crowd at Ken's Grill.

Truth be told, the folks on television are just folks that weren't good enough to work for a newspaper. Sure, it pays more and you get to be on the TV every night, but an empty suit does not a newscast make.

The breakfast crowd at Ken's is an indispensable source of news. We've tried several times to infiltrate their group, but we've yet to get one of our own into their inner circle. The last reporter we sent out there never came back.

"We don't know what happened to him, but we believe somebody slipped something into his orange juice," Paulette Burroughs of The Free Press said. "Rumor has it he sometimes dresses up like the Statue of Liberty and waves at motorists on Vernon Avenue."

That leaves us with our biggest competitor, the Internet.

In the spirit of full disclosure, I admit that I read the news on the internet. (www.Kinston.com). Back when I had the time to sit back and spend a few minutes reading the paper, I enjoyed it. Now, pretty much every minute of the day has an assigned task, so the immediacy of the internet is appealing.

While that immediacy is convenient, it cannot compete with what The Free Press has in store for its paper edition.

The same company that owns The Free Press also owns the Lowenstein Vitamin Company of greater Nicaragua. Due to the economic downturn and the fact that oranges are in plentiful supply down there, the vitamin C division has been shut down.

Although the company will no longer be manufacturing vitamin C tablets, there is an enormous amount of powdered vitamin C sitting in a silo in Central America.

Seeing an opportunity, content editor Bryan Hanks recently struck a deal to start mixing the vitamin C powder into the ink that is used to print The Free Press.

"We've been told to come up with ways to make The Free Press more attractive as a product," Hanks said. "What's great is that if you wrap fish in it, it actually makes the fish more nutritious."

For years we've learned to hold newspapers by the edges to avoid getting ink on our hands. Now, we have to make a conscious effort to get as gommed up in ink as possible.

"If you see someone at work with ink all over their face, normally you'd think they had rickets; now, it's just a sign of good common sense," Hanks said.

The ink/vitamin hybrid, known in the industry as "vitamin zink", still has to be approved by the FDA.

The FDA could not be reached for comment, so we asked the crazy man that hangs around the Kinston courthouse what he thought.

"Shoot man, I've been lickin' newspapers for years," Crazy Courthouse Man said. "You can't beat a sardine and newspaper sammich."

"OCTO-MOM" HEADED TO KINSTON
MARCH 03, 2009

Nadya Suleman, the Californian mother of 14, is headed for Kinston.

A spokesman stated Suleman - who recently gave birth to octuplets - chose Kinston for a practical reason.

"Kinston has more all-you-can-eat buffets than any other city in the United States," Suleman's publicist said. "She's planning on starting her own baseball team, so they're going to need plenty of chow. She also heard that Paulette Burroughs was under house arrest, so we figured it'd be easy to talk her into babysitting."

While I'm sure some folks will think it's cute that this nutjob is moving to Kinston, I'm a bit frightened. That is why, instead of trying to write a funny column, I'm going to use this space to give Ms. Suleman some advice.

First of all, it's a womb, not a clown car! You have got to stop having children. I know Angelina Jolie has 30 kids, but she makes about about 10 million dollars a day, so she can afford to super-size all of those Happy Meals.

Secondly, I think you'll need a day care license to have that many children in your home. That leads one to wonder if you'll have to charge yourself money for keeping your own children. With all of those kids, I'm assuming you don't have time to work, so I'm also assuming you'll be getting some sort of government support to help pay for daycare.

If it gets out that the government is paying you to keep your own children, it could rub some folks the wrong way.

Another issue is shopping. With all of those kids, Kinston would have to bring in another Wal-Mart just to provide retail services to your family. This may sound like a good idea, as a new Wal-Mart would bring new jobs to Kinston.

But when your children realize their mom's grits aren't cooked all the way, they will assuredly run away in the middle of the night. When this happens, we'll be stuck with an empty building and more unemployed people.

The stimulus package that just passed through our intestine-like maze of government was supposedly intended to help a large number of Americans, not just crazy people who wanted to create their own private touring company of The Waltons on ice.

Ms. Suleman, your package has been stimulated quite enough; it's time to shut it down.

KINSTON MUSICIANS STEAL ENTIRE HOTEL ROOM
MARCH 10, 2009

Columnist's note: The following story is true. The names have been changed to protect the guilty.

On a Friday morning in 1996, I woke up in a hotel room in Wilmington, surrounded by blood.

We had played a show at a hotel bar in Wilmington the night before and we were headed to Charlotte the next morning. After the Wilmington show, we got our money, filled up on free soda and Chex mix and headed back to our complimentary hotel room.

Since we weren't exactly staying in the financial district, we took all of the equipment and loaded it into the hotel room. Our theory was that if somebody was going to steal our stuff, they'd have to listen to us snore while they did it.

Now we had just spent three hours staring at two rows of bright lights, so the only light we turned on in the room was the television. We sat around watching TV until the wee hours and we eventually fell asleep.

Being the only farm boy in the group, I was the first one to wake up. I pulled the sheets back on the bed and saw a blood stain on the mattress that was as big as a dining room table.

I immediately hollered and started checking to see which one of my kidneys was missing. This awoke my bandmates, who opened their eyes to find me checking myself for a knife or gunshot wound.

After I realized that I wasn't bleeding, I jumped in the shower and stood under the scalding hot water for what felt like an hour. I tell you, I've never scrubbed so hard in all my life.

I got dressed, and we all went down to the front desk. I told the manager that I woke up to a blood-stained bed. The manager, with a straight face, looked me square in the face and asked me the following question, "Well, are you bleeding, sir?"

At this point, the other guys in the band started physically restraining me. One of the guys, Kinston musician Jode Haskins, asked the manager to come down to the room and see for himself.

We all went back down to the room, and there it was, a giant, red blood stain in the middle of the bed. It looked like somebody was painting a stop sign and forgot the white paint. This thing was huge.

"Well sir, I don't know how that got there; are you sure you're not bleeding?" he asked AGAIN.

With that, I started to undress in front of the guy and show him that I had not been stabbed, shot, or bitten.

Then, they brought in the cleaning woman that had "cleaned" the room the day before. She walks in the room, looks at the stain, and with the calmest demeanor this side of Floyd the Barber said, "I guess I missed it yesterday; are you sure you're not bleeding, sir?"

By this point, I'm on the phone with the police, because I think I've woken up in a murder scene.

"Well, is there a body at the scene?" the dispatcher asked me.

"Not any dead ones," I said.

"If they find a body, have the manager call us back," the dispatcher said. "We'll also need your name and phone number in case something comes up."

I told the dispatcher my name was Buddy Ebson, and I gave him the phone number of an ex-girlfriend from high school.

The manager, who was now threatening to have us arrested for disturbing the peace, told us we had 30 minutes to leave.

I jumped in the shower, scrubbed under the scalding water for a few more minutes and we headed down the road to Raleigh.

We never found out what happened in that room, but I'm still enjoying the TV, towels, table, chairs, telephone, light fixture, sink, carpet, and air conditioning unit that we stole from that room.

P.S. All of you Paulette fans out there, let's get that $25 in for the United Way.

FREE PRESS REPORTER BANNED FROM LOCAL PLANT
MARCH 17, 2009

The first time I was banned from a business was back in 1999.

It happened shortly after my tenure as a desk jockey at DuPont. I'd worked there for about 18 months in an office that was originally a bathroom.

No kidding! The drain was next to the fax machine, and in the summer when the temperatures rose, aromas from times past roared back to life with a vengeance.

I eventually tunneled out and found employment elsewhere, but I would occasionally stop back in to visit some of the shift managers, as they were all pretty good folks.

One night I stopped by the plant with a box of chicken for a friend of mine who was still a shift leader. For the sake of this column, we'll refer to him as Larry.

Larry met me at the gate and got me through security. We went back to the old toilet/office and tore into that fried chicken like two jackals. It was good and greasy and honestly, it looked like a crime scene by the time we were finished.

After we caught up on company gossip, I thought it would be funny to send an e-mail to the company president from my old business e-mail account.

I spent the next half-hour composing a lengthy e-mail that detailed how the managers on the site were making their secretaries walk around in bikinis. Of course, this wasn't true, but at 2 a.m., Larry and I thought it was really funny.

Fast forward to a few weeks later: Larry called me with a real sense of panic in his voice.

"Whatever you do, act like that e-mail never happened - pretend you didn't come by here last week - DENY, DENY, DENY!" Larry said.

As it turns out, the president of the company was a man of advanced years who didn't realize the whole thing was a joke. As told to me by several people, the president of the company called my old boss and asked why he was letting women walk around the plant in bikinis.

In fact, he made a special trip to the plant to investigate what was going on.

I started getting phone calls from people that wouldn't even give me the time of day when I worked there. I mean, these folks had their names on their parking spaces.

"Hi Jon, this is Blabity Blah, and we were calling to ask about an e-mail that made it all the way to the president of the company. Please call us back."

I never called, as I was laughing too hard.

Epilogue: Within days of Bikini-gate, an order was issued that I, Jon Dawson, was banned from every DuPont plant on Planet Earth. I still have the company e-mail framed above my desk: "From this day forward, former employee Jon Dawson is banned from all sites owned and operated by DuPont."

This was the first time I was banned from a business. The second time it happened was last week at the Kinston Country Club; more on that later this week.

PEARSON AND DAWSON SHIELDED US FROM EVIL
APRIL 09, 2009

I spent most of Wednesday at the Lenoir County Sheriff's Office gathering information about the shooting that took the life of Detective Allen Pearson and wounded Detective Ryan Dawson.

While the courthouse is typically a government building full of officials doing official things, on Wednesday it was transformed into an extended family grieving the loss of one of their own.

Because of my job, I visit the courthouse every morning. I see many of the same faces everyday. One of the faces I see often is that of Maj. Ricky Pearson Sr., Allen Pearson's father.

When I got the news that Allen had been shot, I - like most people - developed a knot in my stomach and shoulders. As much as I tried to block it out, the only thought that kept running through my head all morning was of Maj. Pearson getting the call that his son had been shot. As much as I tried to make the thought go away, it just wouldn't.

After writing the basic information pertaining to the shooting, I went to the courthouse to talk to some of Allen's colleagues. The people I spoke to - both on and off the record - were full of despair, anger, and helplessness. As Maj. Chris Hill said when I interviewed him, reality had slapped the entire sheriff's office in the face.

Wednesday afternoon, I asked someone in the department who was close to Maj. Pearson to contact the family and ask if Allen's father would mind making a statement about his son. I've got to tell you that I felt extremely uncomfortable doing that; but it's part of my job description, so I did it.

Initially, the family member said that Mr. Pearson just wasn't up to talking - which I understood. To be honest, I was actually relieved, as I didn't know how I would be able to talk to this man without breaking down myself.

A few minutes later, Jackie Holland of the LCSO told me that Maj. Pearson changed his mind and asked me to visit his home. The thought of intruding on this family during their grieving made me feel extremely uncomfortable, but the feeling that I should honor Mr. Pearson's request was stronger, so I went.

As I walked into the Pearson's home, the feeling that I was intruding was almost overpowering. I just kept wondering how I would react to a reporter being in my home if this had happened to me.

Maj. Pearson was talking to someone, so I just stood in the kitchen for a few minutes and just tried to stay out of the way. I wasn't there long before a family member handed me a glass of tea and a plate of food. I told the family member that they would need this food for the family, but they politely told me that I was going to eat something like everybody else, so I did.

When he finished talking to a well-wisher he looked at me and quietly said, "Are you ready?" I really wasn't, but I nodded yes and started talking to him about his son.

I sat down at the dining room table across from Maj. Pearson. You could tell by looking at his face that he was going through hell, but his reputation for being tough proved true. He sat there and spoke fondly about his son with his family and friends. I swear to God I don't think 10 professional football teams could muster the amount of strength Maj. Pearson displayed while talking about his son yesterday.

When our conversation was over, I thanked him and his family for letting me talk to them and went on my way. Out in the yard, a fellow officer pointed at a pack house across the field and said that if a gunman was hiding in that barn, Allen would have headed in there after him without even thinking about it.

The person that shot Allen Pearson and Ryan Dawson has been written about enough, so I'll not mention his name here. I will say that we should all we should all thank God that these brave officers - for whatever reason - are driven to protect us from evil. If these officers hadn't intervened Tuesday night, who knows what other profane acts this lunatic would have committed?

Most of us would lay down our lives to protect our family, but how many of us would do it just because it was the right thing to do? Could you do it?

SEWER TROUT BUSINESS COMING TO KINSTON
MAY 05, 2009

While the hopes of jobs from the likes of Sanderson Foods and Spirit AeroSystems have left Kinstonians twisting in the wind, a new company is preparing to set up shop in our town.

On Wednesday, Canadian-based Sewer Trout Enterprises is expected to announce plans to build a fishery within the city limits.

"Sewer trout are very popular in Canada," said company Vice President Jeffrey Runyon. "We believe Kinston is a good place to see how Americans will react to our business model."

Sewer trouting's origins can be traced to Montreal in the 1980s. When young people from rural areas of Canada migrated to metropolitan areas for colleges and careers, they missed the ice fishing days of their youth.

"A couple of drunk college students decided they wanted to go ice fishing one night," Canadian historian Scott Moeser said. "They were going to college near Montreal, so there were no frozen ponds."

Moeser said that, in their alcohol-induced state, they acquired some fishing rods, removed a couple of manhole covers and started fishing in the middle of the street.

"These guys were arrested within minutes, but the legend of what they did grew, and before you know it, college kids all over Canada were going sewer trouting," said Moeser.

In 1996, a group of business majors, terrified at the thought of having 9-to-5 jobs, pooled their money to start Sewer Trout Enterprises.

Runyon said in a few weeks F.H.S. (Fish Husbandry Specialists) will begin populating Kinston's sewer system with speckled trout.

"I haven't heard of anything like this since the old Frosty Morn plant was in town," said James Morrison of Snow Hill. "They used to dump the meat scraps in the river, and the catfish knew to wait for it every day."

Morrison said truck drivers who were waiting for their trucks to be unloaded would go behind the plant with a fishing pole and come back with catfish the size of a Pontiac.

"They were pretty big fish, but if you rubbed two of them together, they'd catch on fire," Morrison said.

Community leaders think sewer trouting could stem gang violence.

"I would like to start a guns-for-poles program," says noted in-activist Jasper Arbuckle of Kinston. "It will be a glorius day when the Crips and the Bloods sling bait instead of lead."

For their part, Sewer Trout Enterprises is doing everything they can to protect potential customers.

"Obviously, if you're going to go fishing in the middle of Vernon Avenue, you should take precautions," Runyon said. "We'll be selling disposable flurescent orange fishing suits for $99.95."

According to its Web site (www.bucklesberry.com), Sewer Trout Enterprises will be selling special sewer trout fishing licenses at participating gun shops and beauty salons.

While the thought of new jobs is encouraging, Maj. Greg Thompson of the Kinston Department of Public Safety says the new business could be problematic.

"I like fishing as much as the next guy, but sending citizens into traffic with fishing poles could create an awful lot of paperwork for our officers," Thompson said. "We have enough trouble with people getting hooked on things around here as it is."

LA GRANGE IS THE ALL-AMERICA CITY
MAY 12, 2009

For about a month now we've been debating whether or not Kinston should apply for All-America City status.

Actually, you all have been debating; I've been selling Bryan Hanks' pinky ring collection on eBay.

With all the ranting and raving about Kinston, I have to ask: Why not La Grange?

Seriously, what does Kinston have that La Grange doesn't?

Kinston has a mall; La Grange has a flea market. They both have about the same amount of stores in them, and there are no stores in the mall that have the complete Mel Tillis catalogue on 8-track cassette or a bag of used underwear for $1.

Kinston has a minor league baseball team, but La Grange has a Little League field and a softball field.

Had you rather watch an endless stream of professional baseball players make perfect plays, or had you rather see an 8-year-old hit the ball and run to third base?

Kinston has a Bojangle's, as does La Grange. What makes the La Grange Bojangle's better? It was originally built backwards, which makes it a tourist attraction.

Kinston has an arts council, as does La Grange. While the Kinston Arts Council is open for most of the week, the La Grange Arts Council is only open one day per week - but if you go up to the window and stand on your tip-toes, you can see a few pictures.

Besides, if you visit an art gallery more than once per week, you're just showing off.

La Grange deserves its moment in the sun. The only road block facing the town is the $35,000 that it will cost to send a delegation to Florida to compete for the award.

Would La Grange be able to raise the $35,000 for the trip to Tampa? I'm not sure. I tend to believe the folks in La Grange would realize that $35,000 could do more good if it was used to buy better equipment for emergency personnel, improve its roads and buy all of its public school teachers a bulletproof vest.

Heck, buying 35,000 lottery tickets would be a more responsible use of the money. At least there would be a chance of a return on the money.

FREE PRESS NOW PRINTED ON POTATO SKINS
JUNE 03, 2009

By now, you may have noticed The Free Press has lost some weight. The paper doesn't look like it used to, but to those of you who are in your 13th hour of cow labor, let's look at what this new format means for you.

For starters, a smaller paper means that your garbage can will take longer to fill up, thus reducing your trips to the dump, which will save money on gas. Right off the bat, The Free Press is saving you gas money and reducing the harmful carbon dioxide gases that are threatening our very existence.

Also, the new paper is not actually printed on paper. Instead, our parent company struck a deal with Wendy's restaurant chain to recycle used potato skins.

That's right, this paper that you're currently reading was printed on compressed baked potato skins collected from area Wendy's restaurants.

Once you've finished reading The Free Press, simply place it in an oven for an hour at 400F. Once you remove it from the oven, mix in butter and sour cream. The Tuesday and Thursday editions will also consist of cheese, thanks to the inclusion of my columns and reviews.

The color ink used in the paper is now extracted from discarded jelly, mustard and ketchup packets, so please sample your paper before adding salt or other condiments. Nothing infuriates a cook more than someone dousing food with salt before tasting it.

Another new feature we're introducing is an audio version of the paper. For those of you who don't have time to read the paper or visit www.Kinston.com, you can now call The Free Press and Paulette Burroughs will read the paper to you over the phone.

If you just want the sports section, Bryan Hanks will actually sing it to you in the style of Julie Andrews. If you want him to wear his little Captain von Trapp outfit, it will cost extra.

Epilogue: Sadly, on Monday morning we got word that there was a problem with the new printing equipment. It's similar to getting a new television: You know the new TV is better than the old one, but it might take a day to master the remote.

Hang in there dear readers, for if not for you, I would be forced to return to my previous job as a male model.

And no one wants that.

THE DEVIL WENT DOWN TO KINSTON
JUNE 09, 2009

The Kinston Town Council recently voted 3-2 to annex a chunk of the county, which as I understand it, is illegal in 48 states. Sure, prostitution is still legal in parts of Nevada, but that doesn't make it right.

There is a growing movement to stop this blatant grab for more tax dollars, and every social movement needs its own song. To help out, I've reworked a couple of classic songs will hopefully act as a rallying cry against this mafia-esque form of manifest destiny.

"The Devil Went Down To Kinston," sung to the tune of "The Devil Went Down To Georgia" by The Charlie Daniels Band:

The devil went down to Kinston, he was looking for some land to steal.
He was in a bind 'cos of real tough times - he was willin' to make a deal.
When he came across this town council in a meetin' that was gettin' hot.
The devil jumped up to the podium and said, "Councilmen, let me tell you what.
I bet you didn't know it, but I'm a land developer too.
And if you'd care to take a dare, I'll make a bet with you.
Now you've got a pretty big city here, but give the devil his due:
I bet a fiddle of gold against your town, 'cos I like taxes just like you."
The council said: "We represent the city, and it might be a sin,
But we'll take your bet, your gonna regret, 'cos annexation is about to begin."
The council took a vote, and it fell down 3-2.
The city wants the golf course and Castle Oaks, it's true.
The county hired a lawyer, so their lives they wouldn't lose
If they don't win, they'll surely up and move.

"Your Land Is Our Land," sung to the tune of "This Land Is Your Land" by Woody Guthrie:

This land was your land
But now it's our land
From Highway 70
To the Bethel corn fields
Castle Oaks is next, Lord - and then the golf course
Kinston has deemed to steal this land
Our town is surely circling the drain
We need your dollars to ease our pain
We'll take your land, now
Please don't complain, dears
Your land was made to give to me

There you have it folks. Grab those guitars and tambourines and take to the streets. If the annexation goes through, I've got all the contact info for U-haul right here on my desk.

DAWSON DELIVERS COMMENCEMENT ADDRESS
JUNE 23, 2009

I was recently hired to deliver the commencement address at a local high school. Everything was set until some uppity school board member threatened to "burn down the gymnasium" if I was allowed within 100 yards of the campus.

Long story short, the school board caved, AND they asked me to return their check.

I tell ya, I got a good laugh over that one.

Since I labored a good 13 minutes on the commencement speech, I've decided to print it here:

"Dear graduates, teachers and parole officers, I come here today not to lecture, but to enlighten. I have experienced many ups and downs during my time on this spinning blue ball, and my goal is to prepare you for what lies ahead.

For those of you who are thinking about going to college, I suggest that you attend a community college for the first two years. All colleges require you to take the same courses your freshman and sophomore years anyway, and it will save a large amount of money. After your two years of community college are done, take all of the money that you were going to spend on a four-year school, put it in the bank, and find a job. Take it from somebody that's been there, unless you're planning on becoming a doctor, lawyer or Wal-Mart greeter, those last two years of college are fairly redundant.

For example, at the ECU School of Business, they spent two years cramming something into my head called 'TQM.' Sounds impressive, right? 'TQM' stands for Total Quality Management, which means that instead of inspecting a product when it's finished, inspect it at each stage of its assembly. Basically, ECU has created a two-year program that teaches hundreds of 20-somethings to check their work as they go and they're charging several thousand dollars for that information.

Let me save you some dough: If you do something, make sure you're doing it right while you're doing it. I just saved you two years of college and thousands of dollars. You're welcome.

Once you get that degree, you're going to feel like the world is your oyster. But after a few dozen job interviews that go nowhere, the world will start to smell like an oyster; an oyster that has been sitting in a styrofoam container in the backseat of your car for three days.

On more than one occasion, a prospective employer looked me straight in the face and said, 'Well, you have a degree, which means you'll want too much money or you'll leave as soon as you find something better, so we're going to pass.'

After a while, I started removing the ECU portion of my education history from my resume, leaving only the two-year degree from Lenoir Community College. Within days, I started getting better interviews, and I eventually got a job riding a desk in a converted bathroom at a local manufacturing plant.

If you insist on going through with the college thing, you'll spend a lot of your time working on group projects. I'll go ahead and tell you that, short of a root canal with a rusty pitchfork, working in groups will be one of the most painful things you'll ever experience.

With a group project, one or two people will end up doing all of the work, while the other folks do virtually nothing. You'll stay up all night working on the project, and when you get an A on the project, you'll have to share it with the bozos that didn't do any work.

Come to think of it, that's a pretty good lesson on how life really is.

I take it all back; college is worth every penny."

KINSTON WAS BUILT ON NICOTINE AND POLYESTER
JUNE 25, 2009

There have been stories, testimonials and a few fisticuffs that have come about because of Kinston's new All-America City title. Some folks think it's a good thing, some folks think it's a bad thing, and some folks - like myself - could give a tinker's cuss.

The bottom line is that no tax money was used to fund the trip to Tampa, so if it was a waste of time, at least it wasn't a waste of taxpayer money. If this All-America city title sparks some kind of Kinstonian renaissance, then the folks that spearheaded the All-America movement should be hailed as geniuses.

But until history has time to digest what has happened, there is no need to spend a large amount of time pointing fingers or patting backs - time takes time, so just sit back and see what happens.

As I remember it, the two mainstays of the Kinston economy when I was growing up were tobacco and DuPont. I grew up working on a tobacco farm, and in the days before bulk barns, every so often there would be a day off.

Occasionally - on those days off - I would ride to Kinston with my granddaddy and uncles to sell tobacco at Knott's Warehouse. If the tobacco sold for a good price, we'd stop and get a hamburger on the way home. If the tobacco sold for a great price, we'd go nuts and get a $5 steak at the Western Steer that used to operate near LCC.

Like it or not, tobacco farmers built this town. If you could go back in time and subtract tobacco from the equation, then Kinston would be nothing more than a pit stop between Raleigh and the beach; or has that already happened?

I mean, there used to be a tobacco leaf on the entrance to the mall! I remember seeing politicians court farmers with promises of "We'll look out for y'all in Raleigh!"

Nothing makes me angrier than seeing a Yankee lie with a fake Southern accent.

As a side note, please don't waste your time and mine by writing to tell me how awful cigarettes are - anybody that doesn't know cigarettes are bad for them in this day and age shouldn't be allowed to drive a car, vote or procreate. Fried chicken and women can be bad for you too, but - good grief - could you imagine life without either one?

The other pillar of Kinston's economic glory days was DuPont. There is no telling how many houses, cars and educations were bought with money earned by workers at DuPont. The downside is that folks who went to work at DuPont straight out of high school were in a bit of a pickle when the plant started laying workers off like a bodily function about a decade ago.

I worked out there briefly, and to this day I'm not really sure what they were manufacturing while I was there. Some say it was kevlar, some say it was the white stuff that goes in Twinkies; either way, the nutritional value is about the same.

After this country started treating farmers like rented mules, DuPont was the last bastion of non-governmental solid employment in this town. I saw many hardworking men have to give up farming and go to work at DuPont, only to see DuPont shrivel down to almost nothing.

A couple of large businesses have announced plans to bring loads of jobs to Kinston and we're all waiting with bated breath to see if it actually happens. All America city or not, tobacco and DuPont must be replaced before any kind of tangible recovery is going to take place.

THE KING OF POP MEETS ELVIS IN HEAVEN
JUNE 30, 2009

Remember that bad storm that plowed through here on Friday afternoon? Skip Waters and all of the other local forecasters who haven't been fired because they make too much money said it was caused by a cold front, but I ain't buying it.

I think the atmospheric disturbance was caused by the heavenly meeting of Elvis Presley and Michael Jackson.

On paper, it would seem both of these men have a lot in common. Elvis was a worldwide superstar, had a daughter named Lisa Marie Presley and died young due to complications brought on by a drug probelm.

Michael Jackson was a worldwide superstar, was once married to Lisa Marie Presley and died young (allegedly) due to complications brought on by a drug problem.

They also both left this world as pasty white men.

When Michael passed through the pearly gates Thursday, Elvis had his driver pick Michael up in a Cadillac. When the car reached the Graceland North section of heaven, Michael got out of the car and knocked on the door. Elvis opened the door and invited him in.

"So, you're the King of Pop, huh?" Elvis inquired.

"That's right, ooooooh!" Jackson squealed in his characteristic style while gripping himself in an area I'm not allowed to mention in this family publication.

"What's with the one glove?" Elvis asked. "Fingerprints can still be lifted from the other hand."

Hearing that comment, Michael kicked Elvis in his formidable stomach and moonwalked up the side of his head. Elvis countered with a hip swivel and a karate chop that saw Jackson's nose fly right off his head.

Elvis then looked on in horror as Jackson pulled another nose out of his pocket, attached it to his face and - in the great French tradition - smacked his opponent in the face with his 5-pound sequined glove.

Just at that moment, Ray Charles busted though the door and grabbed them both by the ear.

"You two should be ashamed of yourselves," Ray said. "You're both great artists, so why must you fight?"

MJ and Elvis both knew Ray was right. They shook hands and called a truce.

"Besides, neither one of you would have a career without me," Ray said. "I think I'm going to crash here for a while."

After relaxing on one of Elvis' couches, Ray said, "Michael, since you're the King of Pop, go get me a Diet Pepsi. And here's your ear back."

"How about a Diet Coke?" Jackson asked.

"What'd I say?" Ray said.

Ray then turned his attention to Elvis.

"Elvis, go make me one of those peanut butter, banana and bacon sandwiches you're always talking about," he said.

The three music legends then spent the rest of the day dining on nanner sammiches and Diet Pepsi, which made quite a mess. As Elvis and Michael started to clean up the mess, Ray told them to sit down.

"Don't worry about the mess," Ray said. "Billy Mays will be here in a few minutes."

GOOD LOOKS AND CONNECTIONS TRUMP EDUCATION
SEPTEMBER 01, 2009

As the school systems crank back up, I'm reminded of how much I detested school.

I had several good teachers that helped me along on my rise to the middle: Mrs. Suits, Mr. Holder, Mrs. Kinsey, Mr. Woodyard, Mrs. Pitt — you're all partially to blame.

There is one teacher who e-mails me to tell me how much she despises my column. Personally, I think she's holding a grudge from my senior year when some of us took it upon ourselves to glue her classrom door shut on a Friday afternoon.

Everytime I see somebody working with a hammer and chisel it reminds me of the entire class sitting out in the hall that fateful Monday morning while a maintenance man disassembled several hinges so we could get in the classroom.

The teacher in question made fun of my posture and my accent, so I considered the whole thing a wash.

Within the next few weeks, you students out there will be able to tell who the popular kids are. While in theory there is nothing wrong with being popular, there is no need to feel depressed if you are not popular. In fact, it takes more backbone to go your own way and be who you want to be without worrying if a certain number of people will accept you.

For my entire scholastic career, I never got into boozing, partying or getting high. While this helped keep me out of trouble, it didn't do anything for my social life. I don't know if it's this way now, but if you didn't have a beer, a joint or at least a cigarette in your hand, you might as well be prepared to drive out to the airport and watch the planes land for your entertainment.

I understand that we need to educate our young people, but I think they'd be better off if they were educated on how the world really works from a young age instead of letting it slap them in the face when they turn 22.

In kindergarten, for example, the kids should be told that the better-looking children are going to have it much easier than the more homely kids.

It's not a pleasant subject, but you all know that it's true. If I was good-looking I'd probably have Anderson Cooper's job right now.

We should also cut out this garbage of asking kids what they want to be when they grow up. No kid knows what they want to be when they're 10. When I was 10, I wanted to be the announcer on Solid Gold.

The way things are set up now, you're supposed to declare a major and go into that line of work once you graduate.

For the sake of argument, let's suppose Timmy decides he wants to be a teacher. He goes to college, gets the 48 degrees and certificates you need to become a teacher and two weeks into his first teaching job, he realizes he doesn't have what it takes to be a teacher.

What does he do now? Does he tough it out because he got his degree in teaching and become a bitter person with decent insurance, or does he grow a beard, paint his dog green and open an alligator wrestling farm outside of Daytona?

Education is very important, but education alone will not get you through life. The best way to succeed is to come from a wealthy, powerful family. Ted Kennedy got thrown out of school, ran around on his various wives and caused a woman to drown, yet he was able to represent the great state of Massachusetts in the U.S. Senate for decades.

Now if you or I had pulled 1/10 of the stuff Kennedy pulled, we'd be up for parole in 10 years, no matter how well we'd done in school.

Some final notes to you students out there:

• If you're going to wear your pants down around your knees, there's no need wasting time going to school. You could save the taxpayers a lot of money by just bypassing school and heading straight to Maury.

• If you're from a rich family and you're going to end up with a cushy job anyway, go ahead and drop out. Spend your high school years clubbing and wrecking cars. Better to get it out of your system now instead of when you're running for office.

• There is no need to have any more high school reunions — that's what Facebook is for. If someone you knew in high school doesn't have a profile picture, it probably means they've gained about 600 pounds.

• To all you journalism majors out there: The only two people who've ever made any real money in publishing are Hugh Hefner and Larry Flynt; think about it.

IN MEMORY OF LOUISE, 1930-2009
SEPTEMBER 29, 2009

Last week was a pretty rotten week. As a matter of fact, most weeks in recent memory have been rotten, but last week tipped the rotten gear into overdrive.

The week started off with a Monday morning filled with two homes shot up, a man shot in the "lower back/buttocks" and a man being stabbed in the back multiple times. This is all before 10 a.m. Monday.

The time it took to get that story together pretty much meant that everything else that normally gets done got pushed back — which, in turn, put me behind, which drives me insane.

On the domestic front, my daughter fell victim to a mean old ear infection. How mean was it? From 11 p.m. to about 5 a.m., she was in distress, which meant that I slept for about three hours and her mama slept for maybe one hour.

The next day at the doctor's office, it took four people to hold her still enough for a nurse to tend to her ear. Apparently, I've passed my intense phobia of people in white coats who brandish shiny instruments on to my daughter.

By Thursday, I thought the worst of it was over. I mean, surely the powers that be would give a brother at least one day to catch his breath, right?

Wrong.

On Friday morning, I headed out to my little home office at around 6:15 a.m. I checked my phone and saw that various members of my family tried to call me around 3 a.m. Usually, I place my phone on the nightstand when I go to bed. For some reason, this night I left it in the kitchen.

As soon as I saw the time of the calls, I knew that my Grandma Louise — who'd been sick for quite a while — had passed.

The next few days were filled with food, looking for pall bearers, food, family, food, funeral homes and food. As the preacher visited with the family to go over the funeral service, several stories that I've heard all my life were recounted.

My favorite involves my twin uncles getting into a bucket of tractor grease. They apparently started to paint each other with the grease, only to somehow end up fighting on the dirt floor of the tractor shelter. Louise heard the fuss and called them to the house just as my great grandaddy was pulling up into the driveway.

The story goes that Grandaddy looked at the twins covered in tractor grease and dirt and told Louise that it would be less trouble to get two new children rather than try to clean the two in front of her.

We've got a pretty big extended family with four new members scheduled for release within the next few months. I firmly believe the impending arrivals are what kept grandma going for as long as she did. After the doctors announced there was nothing more they could do for her, she said she was going to try and hold on until the new grandbabies arrived.

Sadly, it was not to be.

I have no proof of what heaven is like, but I tend to believe Louise is there right now working on a quilt or cooking a batch of cheese straws for some upcoming function. If it truly is heaven, she'll be able to kick back with a Coca-Cola — wrapped in a napkin — and watch the HGTV channel until she nods off.

WOULD SOMEBODY PLEASE SMACK
MATT LAUER WITH A GOLF CLUB?
DECEMBER 03, 2009

A few days ago I saw Matt Lauer lead a panel discussion on the Tiger Woods car crash story.

If they were reporting the facts, they would have said that Woods crashed his car into a hydrant, and then they would have kicked it back to Al Roker for the weather, or maybe that minx Meredith Vieira for an expose on breast exams for poodles.

Instead of reporting the facts, NBC devoted around 10 minutes of air time to gossip, hearsay and even a little tabloid fodder.

While this was going on, a strange grinding sound started to overwhelm the speaker in my television. For a minute I thought the old girl was about to take a dirt nap on me, when in reality it was actually Edward R. Murrow spinning in his grave at warp speed.

For a minute, let's pretend this Tiger Woods situation is any of our business — which it isn't.

If we are to believe the gossip that is passing for news, we're to believe that Tiger Woods' old lady caught him playing in the sand trap with somebody else and decided to crack him in the gourd with a 9-iron. While the thought of a gojillionaire getting plonked on the head for running around is pretty funny, it does not warrant 24/7 news coverage, especially in the middle of two wars and a recession.

Another controversy that has sprung from this pseudo news story is that Woods may be getting some sort of special treatment because he has money. While this gives people a harmless place to aim their stored up anger, it's extremely silly. Woods has enough money — which he earned legally — to keep the best lawyers in the business on retainer, which he does. His lawyers have reportedly made sure their client has followed the letter of the law regarding the accident.

Some journalists and Matt Lauer act as if Woods stole the Mona Lisa and drew rabbit ears on her head. He just hit a fire hydrant, folks; it's not the crime of the century.

If it's proven that Tiger did cheat on his wife, I could personally care less. I didn't care about Clinton's romp with Natalie from the "Facts of Life," and the rumors about Bryan Hanks and Hal Holbrook that circulated a few years back didn't interest me in the least.

Besides, how many of you out there in readerland have ever paid a lawyer a couple of hundred bucks to make a speeding ticket go away? Did you get angry with yourself when you used money to make a minor traffic incident disappear? If Matt Lauer and his $3 haircut showed up at your door for a comment, how would you have responded?

I'll go ahead and tell you folks right now that if I ever get two nickels to rub together, I will be breaking laws and hiring people to cover it up on a daily basis. Every non-rich person in the world wants to become rich so they can enjoy the perks of the rich. Besides, what's the point of making a bunch of money if you can't weasel out of the occasional misdemeanor or federal investigation?

Hopefully when this non-story is over, Tiger Woods will go on the "Today" show to give a golf lesson and accidentally pop Matt Lauer in the cranium with a pitching wedge. Now that would be news, and it would be one less obstacle between me and Meredith.

Epilogue: It's now 7-hours after I turned in my column, and I just heard the voicemail that Tiger left on the phone of his alleged mistress. Tiger, you're on your own buddy; I did what I could.

FREE PRESS NOW 100 PERCENT SAFE FOR KIDS
DECEMBER 24, 2009

Life always gets a bit crazy as Christmas approaches, but this past week has been one for the books.

For starters, I wrote a little tongue-in-cheek column about Santa Claus that incorporated the Tiger Woods debacle, and I received two types of responses: Huge belly-laughs and utter disgust.

As I sat at my daughter's Christmas play Friday, a very nice woman in her 70s grabbed my arm and told me how much she enjoyed my columns. Later that day, somebody got on Kinston.com and basically wrote that I was the most evil thing to come down the pike since Adolph Hitler and Paris Hilton.

While I thought it was odd that two people could look at the same thing and have such disparate reactions, I took solace in the fact that the latest school official/student controversy would divert attention from me. While that story did grasp everyone's attention for several days — so much so that we had to shut the bulletin board down — it didn't stop the little Santa column from continuing to fester and transmogrify into this strange creature with half a smile and half a frown.

On Tuesday morning, the Santa controversy was still brewing. While at the courthouse in the morning, three officers stopped me to say how hard it made them laugh, while a lady in the clerk's officer told me how much she didn't care for it.

The maelstrom caused by this column has been so strong that the higher-ups at The Free Press have decided that reporters will no longer report on murders, shootings, beatings or robberies; you know, to protect the children.

Murders will now be referred to as "theft of life," beatings will be classified as "roughhousing" and robberies will be written up as "forced sharing" — you know, to protect the children.

When I got back to the office from my morning rounds, there was a huge basket of cookies waiting for me at the front desk. I opened the card and it was from none other than the world's tallest elf, Santa Claus.

"I read your article and thought it was very funny; too bad some folks have no sense of humor. See you on the 24th! Love, Santa," the note read.

With a chest full of pride, I made the uncharacteristically charitable decision to share the cookies with my Free Press coworkers. I walked around the office and encouraged everyone to get a handful. Bryan Hanks cheated by using a giant foam "We're No.1" hand he got from an ECU game, but I didn't care, because Santa Claus liked me, and all those folks that hated on me were wrong.

About an hour later, I started to feel a little woozy; my stomach was queasy and I was so dehydrated I was unable to summon the tears needed for my bi-weekly payday sobbing session.

I looked around the office and noticed that my coworkers were a little green around the gills as well. Johnny Hussey was hugging a trash can like it was a cheerleader on game day. Chris Lavender ran into the bathroom and barricaded the door shut. The most shocking thing that happened was when Paulette Burroughs poured the moonshine out of her Robitussin bottle to fill it with Robitussin.

After a group trip to the emergency room, we returned to the office with our freshly-pumped stomachs and a new appreciation for Santa. I called his lawyers and told him that I'd write a retraction. They agreed to drop the charges if I agreed to run the following statement in the paper:

"At no time has Santa Claus ever indulged in any extramarital affairs. He has been committed to Mrs. Claus for hundreds of years, and with the exception of a brief period of experimentation in the mid-1970s, the couple have maintained a wholesome, Norman Rockwell-esque relationship."

Let this be a lesson to you kids; if you mess with Santa, he'll make you splorch.

FORMER CHILD ACTOR SEEKS LOVE IN KINSTON
JANUARY 12, 2010

I've decided to use this space this week to do some good. No, I'm not going to put a bullseye in the middle to help your parakeet hit the mark; rather, I'm going to try and bring a little love into the world.

Ashley Mills, 36, of Kinston, needs a date. He recently split up with his girlfriend and as fate would have it, his birthday is Feb. 14.

Normally I wouldn't kick a wet cat over a guy's womanly woes, but if mutual friend John Johnson and I have to listen to Ashley whine about women for one more second, one of us is liable to kill him. Johnson was in the military, so he could probably do it with a paper clip, and I've got a whole box of them in my desk.

The details of Ashley's latest breakup are sketchy to say the least. According to him, the breakup came as a complete surprise.

"It's true — I don't like to go out much," Mills said. "But I laid out a lot of dough for some extra-large Tombstone pizzas; I even invested in napkins."

As of this writing, the female formerly known as Ashley's Boo was vacationing in Afgahnistan and could not be reached for comment.

For you gals out there who are looking for a fixer-upper, then Ashley is the man for you.

Well-groomed and schooled at some of the areas finest public educationamal facilities, Ashley comes from a long line of doctors, lawyers and engineers. Never one to follow trends, Mills blazed his own path in the glitzy world of retail grocery. Since 1991, Millls has been employed at the Piggly Wiggly on North Herritage Street in Kinston.

"He's such a nice young man," one customer said. "I haven't seen a smile like that since Boris Karloff did that ad for Crest toothpaste."

Aside from his rugged good looks Ashley is also a proponet of the Zen lifestyle. His home is totally devoid of such trivial nuisances as cups, bowls or food in the refrigerator. If it weren't for the pile of restraining orders from Burt Reynolds stacked at his back door, you'd swear his house had never been lived in.

While some may find it odd that a man who works at a grocery store has no food in his house, Mills promises the lucky woman that agrees to go out with him on Valentine's Day will be treated to the best that Kinston's fast food industry has to offer.

"I'm not going to lie to you, I know how to treat a woman," Mills said. "I'll Super-Size a combo in a New York Minute, beau."

To assist Mills in financing his newest romantic endeavor, The Free Press has agreed to contribute a booklet of coupons from the summer of 2009 — free of charge.

For more about Mills, here are some nuggets from his 2004 biography, "Whatchutalkin' Bout, Grimace," where he talks about his brief career as a child actor.

"When I was 5, my parents took me to an open audition for this new comedy called 'Different Strokes.' The producers were looking for a young black male to play the part of Arnold. Although I'm as white as a bag of flour, I convinced the talent agent I was an albino. Against all odds, I got the part and was flown out to Los Angeles to shoot the pilot."

Mills continued: "Just as we were about to shoot the first scene, Sherman Hemsley (who was shooting 'The Jeffersons' just across the hall) told the producers that I was, in fact, a bonafide honky. Based solely on Hemsley's expertise on the subject, I was fired on the spot and sent across town to play the part of a pickle in a McDonald's commercial. I was accused of stealing cigarettes from the actor that was playing "Grimace" and was blacklisted from Hollywood forever."

Ashley Mills has led a colorful life but he's ready to settle down. I'd help him myself, but I'm tired ... so very, very tired.

Ladies, I suggest you stop wasting your money on the latest Barney Frank romance novel and head for the Mills.

If you'd like to date Ashley Mills, email me at jdawson@freedomenc.com.

NEWPORTS AND JAM LEAD TO MEMORY LOSS
JANUARY 19, 2010

I celebrated another birthday on Monday.

Most adults look at birthdays as a bad thing, but not me. I've always taken things a little too literally, so I had my midlife crisis while I was in middle school. At the tender age of 12, I got a new haircut, bought a sports car and started dating younger women who only wanted me for my money.

Years of drinking cut-rate milk in public schools brought on osteoperosis by the time I was 16. When I graduated college, I pulled my pants up to my chest, bought some black knee-high socks and moved to a retirement community in Boca Raton. After my 12th girlfriend in as many weeks broke a hip, I decided to move back to North Carolina and give life another shot.

I began my birthday by calling in sick. I told my boss Bryan Hanks that I'd had an allergic reaction to some bad hummus and I'd been plotzing all morning. He told me not to get all schmilkis about it and to get some rest.

In fact, I felt great. I have a great family, a mediocre job and a car that's more duct tape than metal. Life was pretty good.

Since I'd lied my way out of work I decided to lie around the house and watch a little TV. I usually leave for work before the sun comes up, so I haven't seen morning television in years. I flipped around and found Regis and Kathy Lee, and I've got to tell you, that Kathy Lee has gotten hotter as she's gotten older. I think Kathy Lee is around 70, but sitting next to Regis, she could pass for a 39-year-old ex-soap opera star.

I flipped over to The Price Is Right, and boy, has Bob Barker gained some weight. Not only has he gained weight, but he's now wearing the same pair of glasses that Mao Tse-Tung wore in his high school picture. I hope Bob has been spayed and neutered and this sort of thing can be contained.

After a few minutes of TV, I decided to scare up some breakfast. Usually breakfast for me consists of whatever food is leftover in the Free Press conference room from the last meeting of honchos, bigwigs, big shots, heads of state, executives and moguls. Sometimes there will be a platter of day-old pastries in there; sometimes there are only a few pounds of crumbs left on the floor.

Heck, I once found a half-eaten bald eagle in there.

Next, I take the conference room leftovers and mix in 20 or 30 of the ketchup and hot sauce packets that are littered all over the breakroom and microwave it for a few minutes. I then set the concoction outside and usually, within a few minutes, the stench will attract an unsuspecting squirrel or rabbit — which, if cleaned and cooked properly, makes a tasty treat, if you mind the tiny bones and even tinier teeth.

Since I didn't have to stab my breakfast with a Bic pen for a change, I decided to cook myself a gourmet breakfast. I grabbed a large bowl and filled it with butter, cheese, eggs, Corn Flakes, half a stick of Right Guard and mixed it all together.

After breakfast and a quick call to the American Association of Poison Control Centers, I felt refreshed and genuinely glad to be alive.

I decided to celebrate by doing nothing. I haven't had a true day off in months, so I plopped down on the couch with a stack of Nancy Drew books and drifted off into a blissful sleep.

A few hours later, Paulette Burroughs knocked on my door. Apparently she got out of her bond hearing early and came over to help me celebrate my birthday. She had a grocery bag filled with Saran Wrap, jumper cables and a mixture of exotic jellies and ointments.

But like a DVR that's being operated by anyone over the age of 40, my memory has been totally erased. Paulette is gone and all that's left of our afternoon together are five empty jars of blueberry jam and half a pack of Newports.

I don't know what happened here today, but whatever it was caused the goldfish to spontaneously grow feet and run out the door. Happy Birthday to me.

KINSTON MAN FORCED TO ROOT FOR DUKE
JANUARY 21, 2010

Some of you may be familiar with the name Jonathan Massey. I know him through his association with Free Press Managing Editor Bryan Hanks.

Supposedly, Massey assists Hanks when covering certain sporting events, such as the recent GlaxoSmithKline Holiday Invitational in Raleigh. I also have it on good authority that Massey is employed as Hanks' houseboy, personal valet and sock darner.

Little is known about the origins of the Hanks/Massey partnership. Rumor has it that upon entering a locker room and seeing a young Massey standing on top of a toilet while trying to flush the funk off of his funkified feet, Hanks offered the young pup a job as his man Friday.

For those of you who attended ECU, such as me:

Definition of man Friday: n. pl. men Friday or men Fridays — an efficient, faithful male aide or employee (Source: www.thefreedictionary.com).

At first, I was a bit put off by Massey's status as Bryan Hanks' go-to guy. When I first started working at The Free Press, most of my duties revolved around preparing Bryan's meals, securing his bail money, distributing hush money to various escort services, and cross-stitching "Home of The Whopper" into all of his underwear.

All of that changed in 2007 when I uncovered a plot by Osama Bin Laden's cousin — Leroy Bin Laden — to release a collard-fart bomb in Duplin County. The resulting press coverage elevated me to the status of staff writer, which is one notch above the guy that stands under the elephant to see if the diuretic is working, and one notch below the guy who has to shave Rosie O'Donnell's back.

With me out of the way, Jonathan Massey was able to step in and massage himself up to executive assistant status. Of course, it isn't all gravy, and as the great Stan Lee wrote, "With great power comes great responsibility."

Massey — a lifelong UNC fan — had to shield his love of the Tar Heels from his new boss.

"Bryan was cut from the UNC cheerleading squad back in 1946 for trying to milk the ram," Massey said. "Ever since that happened, Bryan has been a massive UNC hater, and requires all of his employees to do the same."

Hanks' blind hatred of UNC forced Massey to sell all of his UNC memorabilia on eBay, including one of his favorite pieces.

"I had a pair of Michael Jordan shrimp straighteners from one of his restaurants in Chicago," Massey said. "I sold them to Free Press Publisher Patrick Holmes, who uses them to pick knots out of uncirculated spandex."

To further the ruse that he dislikes UNC, Massey has stooped to wearing Duke paraphernalia in public.

"When I first started wearing the Duke stuff, I was sick on my stomach for several days," Massey said. "I used to think that Duke fans were born that way — not that there's anything wrong with it — but I must say that after defiling myself in this manner, it has eroded what little self-esteem I had left."

To join the "Free Jonathan Massey From Duke" campaign, contact me via the links below.

UNC/UVA GAME LEADS TO FIGHT IN KINSTON OFFICE
FEBRUARY 02, 2010

Yes, the UNC basketball program is on the ropes this year. For eons, UNC has religiously beaten the snot out of the competition. This tradition of simply being better than everybody else most of the time has left a bad taste in the mouth of UNC's Atlantic Coast Conference brethren.

Bad seasons for UNC basketball come around with the frequency of Haley's Comet, so when the Tar Heels have a bad season, all of the little girlie teams that Carolina has beaten like a rented mule for decades suddenly bow up like like a redneck in a bar fight and decide to take advantage of their 6-minutes of superiority.

The only sport I've ever paid any attention to is ACC basketball. Football, baseball and golf are all reasonably fun to play, but as spectator sports, they are about as interesting to watch as "How Did He Get A Show?: The Jimmy Kimmel Story."

When I talk about ACC basketball, I'm not talking about the current version — I'm old school, baby. I'm talking about the ACC that consisted of eight teams; the ACC that allowed all of the teams to actually play each other twice in one year; the ACC that would howl with laughter at the thought of Boston College becoming part of the conference. Why not just bring in a team from Russia and get it over with?

As far as I'm concerned, the best way to experience a basketball game is to turn the sound down on the TV and listen to the radio coverage. Even Bryan Hanks (who, to his credit, has openly supported the University of Virginia prior to its recent success) even admits that he enjoys the broadcasting prowess and goofball charm of The Voice of The Tar Heels, Woody Durham.

I know most of you out there are obsessed with getting a TV the size of a billboard, but there is just something magical about an old school play-by-play man's voice that is more interesting to me than a TV picture that is so clear you can read the tattoos of the players without having to get out of your chair.

While I've been known to holler or punch something while listening to a game, I've never felt the urge to strip down to my drawers, cover myself in navy blue body paint and jump up and down and scream like an orangutan on PCP for the duration of a game. How anyone could sit next to one of these idiots at Cameron Indoor Stadium and enjoy the game is beyond me.

Take it from someone who processes hundreds of police reports a week: If you or I acted like those Cameron Crazies on Queen Street, we'd be arrested. I understand showing team pride, but really, it's not worth making a complete fool of yourself to support a group of guys that would never hang out with you in real life.

Even The Free Press is not immune to this sort of overzealous behavior. I called Bryan on Monday morning in reference to a crime story, and he was literally choking back the tears after an encounter with everybody's favorite Tar Heel fan, Paulette Burroughs.

According to Hanks — who admitted to wearing a UVA shirt at the time of the incident — he walked up to Paulette and said good morning. But upon seeing his shirt, she turned her head and let several expletives fly.

After hearing this, I called Paulette to get her side of the story, because Paulette has to deal with a lot of customers who are — to put it politely — "full of personality." If somebody's paper is late, wet, or half eaten, Paulette is the one who has to handle the problem, and she usually does so with a smile on her face; so the idea of her attacking Hanks for simply wearing a shirt seemed out of character.

I got Paulette on the phone and her version of events was a bit different.

"Oh he came in wearing this big orange shirt," Paulette said. "Nancy Saunders said he looked like an orange traffic cone."

According to Paulette, Hanks walked into the office with a boombox. He then placed the boombox on the floor, hit the play button, and as the Vince Guraldi music from the Charlie Brown TV specials played, Hanks proceeded to do the Snoopy dance with a life-sized cardboard cut-out of ancient UVa star Ralph Sampson.

"I admit I got a bit testy," Paulette said. "I threw a pencil at him and he went away."

According to Hanks, Paulette jumped over the counter, tackled him, and tried to staple his right ear to his left buttock.

After the ambulance left, Hanks and Paulette begrudgingly shook hands and went their separate ways. For my part, I've decided to remain neutral. Hanks is my boss, and Paulette brings food; either way, I have nothing to gain by ticking off either of these folks.

For my UNC brethren out there, I advise you to keep the faith. When Duke or N.C. State fans berate you about UNC's poor performance this year, just remind them that in the UNC/Duke series, UNC is 33 games ahead, and in the UNC/NCSU series, UNC is 96 games ahead. Even if UNC has 10 bad seasons in a row, we'll still be ahead of you, you petulent little weasels.

Now if you'll all excuse me, I have some whine and cheese to attend to.

TIGER WOODS AND JOHN EDWARDS TO RELEASE ALBUM OF DUETS
FEBRUARY 18, 2010

I'll be heading to the lush tundra of New Jersey in a few weeks to continue work on a new album. As with my band's last album (www.thirdofnever.net), this one will feature John "Rabbit" Bundrick of The Who on keyboards.

Rabbit recently played keyboards with The Who at the Super Bowl and I even did an online video chat with him at noon on Super Bowl Sunday. It was astonishing how relaxed the man was just before playing in front of 190 million viewers; he even took notice of the barbecue that was presented to me while we were chatting.

For about 10 minutes we chatted about the stuff we're working on together and the possibility of a show in Texas next year. After we signed off, I got to thinking about another project that would surely sell through the roof: a John Edwards/Tiger Woods duets album.

Imagine it: A disgraced politician and a disgraced sports hero crooning to the masses. But what would they sing? "Ebony and Ivory" (Stevie Wonder & Paul McCartney); "Maneater" and "Family Man" (Hall & Oates); and "The Other Woman" (Ray Parker, Jr.) would be at the top of my list.

As far as popular music goes, the quality of the music takes a back seat to the marketability: Is it something the twits will Tweet about? Will they look good in the video? Will the people involved mind being scummy enough to qualify as tabloid fodder just as the album is coming out? Do I enjoy asking myself questions? I think I do.

Let's take a few moments and imagine what could happen …

For marketability reasons, the name Edwards/Tiger will be shortened to "E.T.," and the name of their debut album will be "E.T. — Don't Phone Home" in tribute to the phone messages that have dogged these two dogs over the last year.

According to industry insiders, E.T. are planning to sign on Chris Brown as an opening act on their new tour.

"They feel having a guy that was found guilty of beating up a woman open their show will make what they did look not quite so bad," said E.T. tour promoter and father of the King of Pop, Joe Jackson.

At a recent show in Washington, D.C., E.T. were joined onstage by Newt Gingrich and Bill Clinton.

"It was awesome!" said one attendee. "Newt and Bubba got onstage and did a slow jam version of 'Let's Get It On' with John Edwards and Tiger! It was a little creepy but entertaining nonetheless."

Managers for Woods, Edwards, Gingrich and Clinton would not comment on rumors that the four famous philanderers would be touring Europe as "Bill Clinton and the Pre-nup All-Stars" in the summer.

"It would be like the second coming of Milli Vanilli," said John Johnson, President of Washed Up Records. "You know it's true."

"I cried like a baby the day Wham broke up," said Bryan Hanks, President of the Andrew Ridgely Fan Club. "This Edwards/Woods joint could usher in a new era of marginally-talented people being rewarded for bad behavior."

MAN INSISTS ON BEING CALLED 'KAREN'
MARCH 02, 2010

As you folks read this I will be driving back from a fun-filled trip to New Jersey. I shared the car ride with my cousin Gene Sutton who was going to visit his son while I plucked some strings for three days.

The day before we left everybody in Jersey tried to dissuade us from driving up north in the middle of a snow storm. We checked out the weather and decided that as long as we had enough blankets and Nabs in the car, we'd be alright. I did watch the movie "Alive" the night before we left — just in case.

We left Friday morning at 6 a.m. with head full of steam and a bag full of sausage biscuits. Gene's GPS unit was voiced by none other than former NBC newsman Tom Brokaw, so we got a good laugh every time Tom tried to pronounce a street name with an 'L' in it.

For the first half of the trip we saw no sings of snow. At a rest stop in Virginia we saw a "Honk if Bryan Hanks Owes You Money" bumper sticker, and in one frightening incident a guy pulled a gun on us at a gas station.

"GIVE ME YOUR MONEY!" the gunman said.

"BUT I WORK AT A NEWSPAPER!" I said.

"Which department?" asked the gunman.

"I'm a writer," I said.

The gunman's face then fell to a defeated frown.

"Here," he said as he handed me the gun. "You need this more than I do."

With a full tank of gas and a slightly used .38 Special in my pocket we motored on up the East Coast without incident. We did start to get into some heavy snow around Maryland, but luckily for us the temperature hovered just above freezing so the roads never iced up.

We pulled into Highland Park around 2:30 p.m., full of pride that we defied the odds and reached out destination all in one piece.

As we unloaded my bags outside my band mate's house, he was amazed that we'd made such good time while driving through a storm. I told him that country boys could survive, and while doing so I opened the front door of the car and smacked myself right between the eyes. According to my friends, I insisted that my name was Karen for the rest of the evening.

Later that night as I started to regain the use of the left side of my body, I decided to go with our singer Kurt while he walked his dog. We got about 12 feet from the house when I hit a patch of black ice and somehow landed directly on my right knee — the same knee that I landed on while preparing for my 37-point performance at this year's United Way Day of Basketball. We patched my knee together with some WD-40 and some duct tape and went on about our business.

I made it through the next day without breaking anything, although the mixing board in the studio (which was originally owned by Miami Vice composer Jan Hammer) broke down around midnight, our bass player's amplifier exploded and our drummers practice p.a. went the way of the Dodo bird.

Even with all the strife we got some good work done, and I'm looking forward to being home again. If I could just get around having to leave the house once I got there I'd be in good shape.

RARE SPIDER FOUND IN KINSTON OFFICE
MARCH 09, 2010

One thing all newspaper people have in common — along with apparently being allergic to money — is that we tend to leave ourselves notes on little scraps of paper. Phone numbers, e-mail addresses and pawn shop tickets accumulate and create an ecosystem that is fed by ink fumes and the sticky-stuff on the back of Post-it notes. The pile of garb — I mean, important information — on one desk at The Free Press led to a major scientific discovery.

The much talked about but rarely seen Cubicle Spider (Spiderousbreedus ondeskus) is rumored to have first drawn breath around the second or third foot of paper on Free Press Managing Editor Bryan Hanks' desk.

"The discovery of the Cubicle Spider is very significant," said Professor John Johnson of the University of North Carolina at Grifton. "We believe the combination of cheap office supplies, flop sweat and spilled Red Bull created a 'perfect storm' for arachnid procreation; when put under a microscope, that desk looks like Mardi Gras on acid."

Notes and questions also pile up on computers. My e-mail account at work is full of questions from readers of this column, so I'm going to take this opportunity to answer some questions from readers:

- LCC and ECU — majored in animal cosmetology.
- Independent.
- No, it's not a wig.
- Twenty-three.
- No, I'm not a post-op trans-gender that ran out of money during the treatments.
- I have no information on the Chris Lavender/Paulette Burroughs annulment.
- Yes, the Free Press is now actually printed on recycled potato skins.
- No.
- Yes.
- Only with proof of immunizations.

• The terms of the settlement prevent me from commenting on Mr. Holmes spandex business.

• Yes.

• Long walks on the beach, romantic candlelight dinners, and shooting rats in the dumpsters behind Wal-Mart.

• Maybe.

• No.

The spam filter in my e-mail account had apparently kept some important messages from my inbox. Thankfully, I found them in time:

The Carell/Grundy Family Reunion will be taking place Nov. 15th, 2008 at the Wheat Swamp Ruritan Building. If you will be attending please contact Agnes Grundy at 252-527-8402. If you will not be attending you are asked to go get stuffed.

On Dec. 7, 2009, The Tick Bite Reporatory Company will present "The Kinston City Council Land Grab Follies: A Musical." The musical will be performed at the Jon Dawson Center for the Barely Adequate Center on E Street, Kinston.

It feels good to get caught up on things; praise the Lord and pass the chicken.

BOWLES INFLUENCED HELMS' CHOICE OF SNUFF
MARCH 23, 2010

Last Thursday, a contingent of Free Press commanders and staff invaded Chapel Hill to attend the 2010 North Carolina Press Association Winter Institute. In plain English, it means hordes of underpaid journalists gathered to pick up a few awards and run up a huge liquor bill on the company credit card.

I snagged a ride to Chapel Hill with fellow Tar Heel supporter and Free Press Publisher Patrick Holmes. After we drove around the campus at UNC for a few hours, we found a parking spot and began the walk up the hill to the Dean Smith Center — which this season has been dubbed the Trail of Tears.

As we approached the front of the Dean Smith Center, an elderly man was climbing up a ladder with a hammer and chisel. This story circulated last week as a joke, but I actually witnessed it: Due to the Heels' limp performance this season, coaching legend Dean Smith was still trying to pry his name from the arena's entrance.

Just to get it out of the way: Did you hear about the students at UNC not being able to get on the Internet? Apparently, they couldn't get three "W's" in a row.

Once inside the Smith Center, Patrick had to attend a few meetings before the awards ceremony, so I wandered around until I found the NCPA awards stage at the east end of the basketball court. An Internet feed of the NCAA basketball tournament was being shown on a big screen, so I found my way down to about the 20th row from the floor. I would have gotten closer, but an official-looking fellow who was wearing a suit that must have set him back at least $30 held up his hand and instructed me not to come any closer.

"I'm here for the NCPAs," I said. "I just wanted to check out the game on the big screen."

The official said, "Well, we don't want anybody to get too close to the stage until the ceremony starts."

I started to ask Mr. Official if top secret military plans were written on the back of the Kinko's printed award certificates, but I'd only had four hours of sleep the night before so I sat on row 21 — safely away from the highly sensitive "Best Coverage of a Haircut" award packet, where I watched Murray State deep-six my NCAA Tournament bracket.

The reception started at 4:30 p.m., and we were all given two tickets for free glasses of wine. I don't drink, so I sold my tickets to a couple of already-tipsy writers for the Weekly Reflector of Asheboro. After their fourth gallon of wine, they both ran onto the court of the Smith Center and tried to cut down the nets. I asked the security guard why he didn't stop them and he said the nets had dry-rotted from under-usage this year so, no harm, no foul.

After the reception, we all filled our coat pockets with as much food as we could and took our seats. After a spirited welcome by the UNC pep squad and band, the ceremony roared into overdrive with the presentation for the "NCPA North Carolinian of The Year" award. This year's recipient was none other than Erskine "Boom Boom" Bowles.

According to the video montage that preceded Bowles acceptance speech, this man's life is chock full of accomplishments. Apparently, along with being a major fundraiser for Bill Clinton in the early 1990s and recently being appointed by President Obama to make this deficit thing go away, Bowles has many other noteworthy accomplishments:

• 1946 — A precocious toddler, Bowles accidentally helped Percy Spencer invent the microwave when he poured a bag of fertilizer into the back of the family television. When the fertilizer came into contact with the hot vacuum tubes in the television the resulting radiation melted a Baby Ruth candy bar that was sitting on a table on the other side of the room.

• 1952 — At the insistence of Bowles, Jonas Salk added two teaspoons of red pepper to his groundbreaking polio vaccine, which ended up saving thousands of lives.

• 1980 — While vacationing in Wilmington, Bowles noticed a gangly 17-year-old Michael Jordan struggling with his jump shot at a public park. Bowles got out of his car and taught the young Jordan the patented "stuck-out-tongue" jumpshot technique that enabled Jordan to become a superstar.

• 1983 — Convinced U.S. Senator Jesse Helms to switch to low-tar snuff.

After the ceremony, Patrick and I decided to skip the Freedom Communications dinner that was being held at a local Wendy's and head back to Lenoir County. As soon as we got to the parking lot, I realized I'd left my cell phone inside the Smith Center. I ran back inside and scoured the seats for my phone. I found $3 in change and a partially eaten pack of Slim Jim's (in the News and Observer section), but no cell phone.

I gave the security guard my information in case he found the phone and like the 2009/10 Tar Heels, I left the Smith Center in defeat.

We got about three miles down the road when Patrick got the call that they'd found my phone and would be mailing it to me. To celebrate, we pulled into the nearest Burger King drive-thru and got two hubcap-sized hamburgers. After inhaling the burgers we went through the UNC School of Medicine drive-thru and ordered two angioplasties from the 99-cent menu.

With our stomachs full and our hearts freshly inflated we barreled down I-40 with what could be described as suitable aplomb. I plugged my 5,000 song-strong (and counting) iPod into Patrick's car stereo and we played Name That Tune for most of the ride home, although it was marred by Patrick's constant requests for "Muskrat Love" by Captain and Tennille.

It got so bad at one point that he ignited a cigarette lighter and started chanting for it. Somewhere around Smithfield, I gave in and started singing it; so if you thought you heard a grown man with a pronounced Southern accent singing "nibbling on bacon/chewing on cheese/Sam says to Suzie, honey/Would you please be my Mrs./Suzie says yes with her kisses" you weren't having a stroke, though you probably would have preferred to have been.

FAST FOOD KETCHUP CAUSES ANEURYSM
MARCH 30, 2010

I'm beginning to think stupidity is an airborne pathogen.

For evidence, try driving along the stretch of Heritage Street between Hardee's and Lovick's. For whatever reason, grown people who've presumably graduated from a top-notch public school have not figured out that a green traffic light means to GO FORWARD. Apparently, there is a tear in the space-time continuum on the corner of Heritage and Phillips that causes drivers to confuse gas pedals with flaming serpents that should either be avoided or handled slowly and delicately.

Honest to goodness, if you try to drive down Heritage Street between the hours of 9 a.m. and noon, it'll take you half an hour to get through two stoplights. I once saw a 16-year-old boy turn onto Heritage Street at 9:15 a.m., and by the time he made it to the King Street Bridge he was old enough for Social Security. He went from pimple cream to Ben Gay over the course of four blocks.

Our next group of dunderpates are the people who don't cover their mouth or nose when coughing or sneezing. I've watched in horror as grown people — who are allowed to operate vehicles, vote and procreate — stand at our front desk, rare back like Sandy Koufax and sneeze like an elephant with a snoot full of black pepper. If the sun is shining in just right, you can actually see the germs as they exit the nostril — it looks like an illegal border crossing sped up like a Benny Hill routine.

And if the knuckle-draggers don't sneeze, they feel no shame in clamping their thumb on the outer nostril so as to give their index finger enough of a foothold to get up in there and extract a conglomeration of stuff so disgusting your body is trying to expel it.

BONUS: Did you know there is a medical term for picking one's nose? Rhinotillexis; sounds like a luxury car for zookeepers doesn't it?

Like you, I know lots of people who can barely summon enough mental energy to fog a mirror. These are the people that stop 50 feet behind cars at stoplights, text message while driving, and take five minutes to order at a drive-thru (they've got burgers — PICK ONE!). I raise my hand to Charlie Pride, I heard someone ask "How much ketchup comes on that sandwich?"

After witnessing this exchange, I heard a loud pop and blacked out. I then found myself walking down a long, dark tunnel with a tiny shaft of light at the end. When I reached the light, a tall man in a finely-tailored suit led me through the pearly gates. There was a little cafe and I saw my grandma in there with her sewing and a Coca-Cola wrapped in a napkin. My long-deceased bulldog Katie ran up to me and licked my face the same way she did when I was 12. Apparently, the nimrod at the drive through had inadvertently sent me to a better place.

Just as I was about to go offer Marilyn Monroe a light, I awoke to find the manager of the Booger Queen waving smelling salts under my nose. She was beautiful and smelled like French fries; I asked her out but she rejected me when she found out that I worked for The Free Press. She said she couldn't date anyone that couldn't afford a Melancholy Meal at Booger Queen; I protested, but after further investigation it was determined I could only afford a 1/3 of an apple turnover and 1/2 a napkin.

Look, I've never claimed to be the sharpest knife in the drawer — I don't get involved in the health care debate because, quite frankly, I don't understand it. I don't know how or if it'll make things better or worse; I don't know how it's going to be paid for; I don't know if halitosis qualifies as a preexisting condition.

That being said, I try to take into account that there are other human beings on the planet, so I cover my mouth when coughing, I don't take two hours to decide on a $3 hamburger and I don't write notes while driving at high rates of speed. We, as a society, have let these sorts of things go unchecked for too long.

If you let people get away with coughing in your face, before long, they'll think they can annex your land.

CHARLES ANDERSEN IS ONE OF THE GOOD GUYS
APRIL 01, 2010

As reported in The Free Press, allegations have been made involving the Lenoir County ABC general manager. Since it's been reported in our paper twice and upwards of a dozen times on television, I see no need to regurgitate the entire story.

If you were out of town or just learned to read Wednesday, the short version is that the Lenoir County general manager allegedly asked a local restaurateur to alter the items (but not the amount) on the receipt he was to turn into his superiors. Apparently $48.75 worth of drinks was turned in as $48.75 worth of food and coffee.

HOLY MACKERAL! CALL THE NATIONAL GUARD! GET THE BOYS FROM NASA IN HERE! SOMEBODY TEAR SOME SHEETS AND BOIL SOME WATER! GODZIRAAAAA!!

If you could all put down the pitchforks and torches for a minute, I think I can talk you down off the ledge.

There has been a deluge of smack talk regarding this incident on our Web site as a lot of folks seem to think the taxpayers have been defrauded. These folks seem to think the only thing keeping Lenoir County from becoming a socioeconomic supernova is $48.75.

Now the story clearly states that the restaurant manager, Charles Andersen, did not alter his books or his copy of the receipt, thus all of the taxes generated from the sale of the drinks went where they were supposed to go.

To recap, taxpayers — in this case, the purchasers of said hooch — were not defrauded. Did the ABC general manager do something at odds with the rules of his job? Maybe he did. The important question is: Do I care? On the list of things I care about, I'd say this falls somewhere between Simon Cowell's bowel movements and whether or not Howard Stern is an android.

I don't know the ABC general manager, so I'm not going to write about him. The previous sentence may be the most profound thing I've ever written. I admitted my ignorance; therefore I chose to keep my pie hole shut on the matter.

The other person involved in this scenario is Charles Andersen. In the interest of full disclosure, Charles is my friend. I worked for him for several years while I was in high school and college. We shared a mutual appreciation for the band Rush — we even saw them in concert once.

Some of you are already yelling "bias!" — and you would be right. I am a 100 percent unabashed Charles Andersen fan.

Charles created a great work environment for his employees. We were all expected to work, but everyone was treated fairly. If somebody was having a problem — be it a busboy, waitress or cook — Charles would just jump in and help without question.

Not only was Charles a good boss, he was a working boss. He did all of the landscaping, ordered and received all of the trucks and on some nights, did all the cooking. He's the kind of boss that made you want to work hard — I actually witnessed some fairly lazy people work harder because seeing how hard Charles worked made them feel guilty.

I could spend five more pages listing Charles Andersen's attributes, but nobody really wants to read about that sort of stuff. Internet trolls have been unfairly getting on Charles' case, and if that weren't bad enough, local TV stations have camped out in the parking lot of his business.

All of these folks who are attacking Charles on our Web site are apparently perfect; I'm sure not one of them has ever driven over the speed limit, ripped the tag off of a mattress or fibbed on their tax returns.

Personally, I find Charles' candor in this situation refreshing. If it'd been me and I'd already been cleared of any legal wrongdoing, I wouldn't have given one media outlet the time of day. Charles didn't have to talk to anybody, but since he's a good guy, he chose to.

I agree this was news, but it seems like a bit of overkill to devote hundreds of dollars in manpower and airtime to a minor personnel issue that was in the process of being handled anyway. I understand reporting it, but it seems we as a community are so hungry for a scandal that we jumped the gun just a bit.

Charles is a veteran, a family man, and a business man — a good businessman. Take your significant other down to The Barn Steakhouse and see for yourself.

CITY OF KINSTON TO ENACT TAX ON WALKING
APRIL 15, 2010

Starting today, residents of Kinston who try to save money by walking will receive another punch in the groin. According to a source on the City Council who wished to be referred to as "Deepbutt," the new tax on walking has been in the works for quite some time.

"They considered a tax on breathing, but it just wasn't cost effective," Deepbutt said. "To get an accurate reading we'd have to hire 27,000 workers to monitor each residents' air intake, and when 'Dancing With The Stars' is on, the rates would naturally go up."

According to the source, all but one of the council members was in favor of taxing breathing.

"They figured they could hire the entire town to monitor each others breath, thus giving us a 0% unemployment rate and unlimited tax revenue," he said.

According to Deepbutt, residents will be able to avoid the tax by hopping, sliding, scooching or rolling.

"There may also be a loophole for dancing," Deepbutt said. "For those of you who were ridiculed in the 1980s for learning the moonwalk or the centipede, rejoice, as busting either one of those moves will not be taxable under the new law."

"I've lived here all my life," said Julian Brixton of Citizens Rallying against More Indecent Taxes, or CRAMIT, "but it's getting to a point where you can't void your bowels without somebody taxing it."

While Brixton's example of excretory taxation may seem far-fetched to some, Deepbutt said it could become a reality before the end of the year.

"The only thing holding back the fecal tax is that most politicians know they're more full of it than anybody else," Deepbutt said.

If Deepbutt is to be believed, the residents of Kinston will be receiving pedometers in the mail beginning Friday.

Citizens who walk with the assistance of crutches or a walker will only be charged 98 percent of the full tax amount. Seniors on a fixed income will be issued a voucher to purchase a pair of orthopedic roller skates, which are not currently taxable.

"The electronic pedometers will automatically send a signal to Electricities, who will, in turn, charge a $25 administrative fee, a $15 handling fee and a $10 just-because-we-can fee," Deepbutt said.

When contacted by The Free Press for comment, one council member was on vacation, while the other four were seen shoulder-rolling down Queen Street.

Jon Dawson's columns appear every Tuesday and Thursday in The Free Press. Contact Jon at 252-559-1083 or jdawson@freedomenc.com. Due to a new City of Kinston fee on syntax, all future columns will contain no punctuation.

12 HOURS OF LABOR AND ANOTHER
REASON TO STAY HOME
APRIL 27, 2010

Last Thursday morning my wife gave birth to our second daughter, Ava.

Ava's due date was May 2, but according to the doctor, we were to expect her to come as early as April 17.

With the notion of an early arrival in my already-cluttered head, every time the phone rang for the weeks leading up to her arrival, I jumped about 10 feet. We were having the baby in Greenville, and I was in no mood to deliver this baby with a State Trooper somewhere on N.C. 11.

I called my wife every hour for a status update. I forbade her from eating boiled okra and told her which pothole-ridden streets to avoid — which, in Kinston, means pretty much all of them.

On Wednesday night after putting our daughter Emma to bed, my wife sat down in the living room to work on some sewing and I returned some phone calls. At 9:30 p.m., I walked through the living room and was informed that it was time to start raking up straw.

We got Emma to my sisters' house and headed to Greenville, which — at that moment — might as well have been in Canada. I had visions of license checks and dozens of other things that could pop up to slow me down, but luckily, we had a smooth trip. I may have inadvertently shoved a loligagging 1977 LTD into a drainage ditch just outside of Grifton, but if you can't drive any faster than 28 mph on N.C. 11, then you really should consider staying home and watching Judge Joe Brown in HD.

On the way to the hospital, my wife noticed that I was wearing the same green shirt that I was wearing when we headed to hospital with our first kid five years ago. You may call it miserly; we call it forced frugality.

Once at the hospital, we realized the pre-registration we'd gone through a few weeks before must have been some sick intern's idea of a practical joke, as we had to regurgitate every speck of biographical information all over again. I understand that they need our I.D. and Social Security number, but I thought it was rather rude of the attendee to ask my wife repeatedly if I was indeed the father.

After we both passed a polygraph test, they took us to a birthing room that was rather impressive; this room had an adjustable hospital bed, TV, hardwood floors, Jacuzzi, ping-pong table and barbecue pit.

They set us up and after a time the doctor entered the room and joyfully recited Robin Williams' great "AT YOUR CERVIX!" line from SNL, and it took several minutes for everybody — including my wife — to stop laughing. After Mr. Goodscaple was finished with the examination, he told us that we had several hours to go, and that my wife should get dressed and walk around the hospital for an hour or so. With that, the doctor lit up a cigarette and headed to the doctor's lounge on the fourth floor.

My parents were in the lobby, so we walked down there to give them an update (I'd tell you my parents names, but they've repeatedly requested that I not). My mama was prepared for a long night in the lobby, as she'd recently gone through this with my sister and her new son, Brennan. She handed me a pack of Nabs and a Pepsi, and it was honestly the best Nab and Pepsi I'd had since the days of barning tobacco.

Fast forward to 6 a.m. on Thursday. We've now been awake for 24 hours, and the baby has apparently heard about the tax situation in Kinston and decided to stay put. A decision is made at 8 a.m. to do something to set the wheels in motion, which causes the contractions to strengthen with extreme prejudice. At 9 a.m., the doctor came in and asked if I could let him hold a 20 until payday.

With the doctor paid up, he brings in an EMT trainee by the name of Avett. The doctor asked if it's OK for Avett to observe the birth for training purposes, which we agree to under the stipulation that Avett not giggle if I pass out during the birth. I was already getting woozy just listening to the heartbeat, so plotzing out during the berf wasn't beyond the realm of possibility.

It turned out Avett was from New Zealand, although his accent was straight-up Crocodile Dundee. After we talked about AC/DC and Nicole Kidman for a few minutes, the doctor instructed me to grab hold of a leg and the back of my wife's neck and pretend I was playing "Ride of the Valkyries" on an accordion.

At 9:25 a.m. — that's right, 28 hours without sleep — the nurse told my wife how to breathe and push. You'd think both of those tasks would be fairly instinctual, but in fact, there are apparently dozens of ways to do each. During the first set of pushing, the doctor's pager went off. While I would have thrown the thing out the window if I could have reached it, Dr. Feelgood had the sense of mind to relay instructions to his other patient while still perched at the end of the bed like Johnny Bench in the 1976 World Series.

The next half hour was really tough; I've always known that my wife was tougher than me, but good God, what a woman goes through during birth. If you ever want to really get a hold of the population problem, rig it so that men are the ones that have to give birth and the highways will become less cluttered within a matter of months. I split my hand open in three places last year like a microwaved banana and nearly passed out; if I'd had to go through what my wife did on Thursday, you might as well go ahead and get me a reservation at Rouse's in La Grange.

Finally, Ava showed up with a head full of hair and a good set of lungs. The doctor offered to let me cut the cord, but I told him to earn his money as I wanted nothing to do with any cutting of any kind.

The birth was tough and my wife has to take it easy for a while, but she and Ava are doing well. We had our first doctor's visit in Kinston Monday morning, and again the smart-alecky receptionist could barely conceal a snorted laugh when my wife told her I was the father of this beautiful little girl.

She then reminded me that falsifying medical records was a serious offense, and I then reminded her that I had a column to write later in the day, and that if she didn't get with the program I'd tell the world how she paid her way through school as a topless dancer at a truck stop in Arizona.

Ava checked out fine, and, according to the doctor, the only problem he could foresee Ava having was her father.

Anybody that has the misfortune of knowing me really well knows that aside from a periodic journey to the Big Apple for musical reasons, I really, really don't like to leave the house. With the addition of Ava to my life, I'm happy to report that my condition has gone from hermit-like tendencies to full-blown anti-social.

Whenever an obese man with a body odor problem decides to sit right next to you in a waiting room even though there are plenty of chairs in the next row, I won't be there. Whenever a woman blathers endlessly on her cell phone while her malnourished and manner-free children destroy half of a department store, I won't be there. Whenever it takes someone 47 seconds to realize the light has turned green on Herritage Street, I won't be there.

Where will I be? I'll be doing something to make the world a better place, like teaching Emma and her new sister how to make the fart noise with their armpits.

N.C. TERRORIST FOUND BEATEN IN LENOIR COUNTY
APRIL 29, 2010

First off, I'd like to thank everybody for their well wishes in regards to the arrival of our new baby girl. Honestly, I was hoping some cash, presents, scholarships — even a box of Cheese Nips — might show up, but times are tough, so I'll just assume y'all are waiting for payday to get here.

We've got a 5-year-old, so we're not total strangers to the baby bidness. In fact, most of our skills have returned, especially those that fall under the category of consolation. With our first kid, we found out that my wife could not eat collards while nursing, because apparently collards turn mother's milk into gun powder and it upsets the baby. This time around, we've discovered that broccoli is the baby equivalent of being cut off in traffic repeatedly.

The contents of one diaper in particular produced by this sweet little baby on Tuesday were deemed illegal to transport over state lines, and after being turned away from three trash dump sites, I placed the diaper — which, after a while, produced an ominous glow — in a cigar box. The cigar box was then wrapped in aluminum foil and duct tape. After a few minutes the aluminum foil started to melt, so I threw the diaper in the toaster, unplugged the toaster, took it out to my car, and drove around to find a place to dispose of this Pamper full of plutonium.

Not long after I made it to U.S. 70, the diaper started barking at me. In a panic, I drove up to a gas station and attempted to throw the diaper in a trash can located next to a gas pump. I opened the door, but before I could wrestle the diaper out of the car, a seedy-looking figure approached me with a briefcase full of money.

The man was dressed in overalls (or as they call 'em in Bucklesberry, overhauls), sporting a turban and a long beard that the members of ZZ Top would find a bit much. He identified himself as Leroy Bin Laden, and said the contents of the barking diaper reminded him of substances he and some friends had been trying to "import" for years.

Being a proud American, my first thought was to kick Leroy in the kiwi's and haul him to the nearest FBI office. Sadly, we just found out this week that all Free Press employees would be paid with Goody's coupons until further notice, so I agreed to sell Leroy Bin Laden the violently odoriferous barking diaper for $5,000.

Leroy reached into his overalls for a pair of isotope holders, but when he attempted to pick the diaper up, it reared up and bit him on the face. For the next 10 minutes the Gailord Sartain of the Jihader Done movement ran around the parking lot of Mallard Food Shop No. 32 with a barking diaper chewing his face off.

Eventually, the diaper got tired and crawled back into my car. Leroy, though beaten and battered, had the piece of mind to ask for his money back. Downtrodden and running low on gas, I decided to confide in my boss, my mentor, my dawg, my boy — Bryan Hanks, Managing Editor of The Free Press. I drove to Bryan's house only to find a note on the door that read, "Gone to Madame Alexander doll auction; be back soon."

At the end of my rope and out of ideas, I autographed the diaper "Best Regards — Mike Krzyzewski" and left it in his mailbox.

LA GRANGE WOMAN GIVES INFANT
CIGARETTES, TATTOO AND MOUNTAIN DEW
MAY 13, 2010

Today, my daughter Ava turns 3-weeks-old. Her entry into this world was pretty hard on my wife, so I decided to take her out for Mother's Day.

As anybody who reads this column with any frequency knows, I usually don't make a big deal out of holidays, as I view most of them as a way to make millions of dollars for the card, candy and hard liquor conglomerates. Add to that the fact that the average Free Press writer is paid less than a Wal-Mart greeter in Ethiopia and you've got yourself a conscientious holiday objector.

(Writer's note: I just spelled "conscientious" without the aid of spell check — Assistant Managing Editor Nancy Saunders is a witness).

I told my wife to get all gussied up, as we had reservations at Hardee's for 7 p.m. My parents volunteered to keep our 5-year-old Emma, and Free Press Human Resources Manager Paulette Burroughs volunteered to look after 3-week-old Ava. We dropped the kids off and headed into town for a night of fine dining at the restaurant that took the least amount of gas to get to. The curly fries were sublime, and the fountain Sprite was a precocious little number from April of 2010; its bouquet was fruity yet manly.

After a great meal, we had the economy version of Bananas Foster (a char-grilled banana split) and headed out to pick up the kids. We picked up Emma from my parents' house and then headed to Paulette's to get Ava.

When we got to Paulette's, Ava was asleep. She looked so sweet wrapped up in her blanket. We thanked Paulette and headed home. About two minutes into the car ride, Ava started belching with extreme prejudice — one of them was so strong the airbag deployed. We couldn't figure out what made her so gassy, so we called Paulette for an explanation.

We got on the phone with Paulette and she said that she'd let Ava have a few sips of her Mountain Dew. When asked if she thought it was a good idea to feed a 3-week-old baby a highly carbonated drink loaded with corn syrup,

Paulette said they used to use it as a substitute back in the day when the wet nurse called in sick.

Cramming the airbag back into the steering wheel was really tedious, as our car is a late 1990s model that was equipped with an airbag that consisted of used packing peanuts and several gallons of fat that had been liposuctioned from Robin Quivers' head.

Once in the house, we noticed a square bulge under Ava's shirt on her left arm. We unrolled her shirt to find a tiny box of unfiltered Camel cigarettes. We called Paulette and asked why our 3-week-old had a partially smoked box of Camel cigarettes tucked under her shirt, Schneider-style.

"I thought she was too young for a whole carton," Paulette said. "That would have been irresponsible."

We ran a bath and got Ava out of her clothes, only to find a tattoo on her right arm that read "Bocephus" and one on her left arm that read "Thug-4-Life." We got on the phone again to Paulette and asked about the tattoos.

"I had a coupon for Emit and Earl's Ice Cream and Tattoo Parlor," Paulette said. "I figured the tattoos were the better investment since they would last longer than the ice cream."

After an evening that could be the basis for an awful Drew Barrymore romantic comedy, there was a knock on the door. I opened the door to find an 8-week old boy standing there with the aid of a baby walker. He was a bit of a punk — he was wearing his bib sideways and his diaper was riding so low that half his butt was sticking out.

The punkfant handed me a Blackberry with a text message stating that he wanted to take Ava out on a date. I asked him how he knew my daughter, and he said he met her at a Tupperware party at Paulette's house.

As I wrapped Minimem up in a towel and set out to find his mother, I found a tattoo on his leg that read "If lost, return to The Home for Children That Might Have Been Fathered by John Edwards."

To be continued.

(Happy Birthday Lolas Blizzard!)

FIRE DEPARTMENT ASSISTS IN PROSTATE EXAM
MAY 18, 2010

You wouldn't know it by looking at me, but up to this point I've been blessed with good health. People who know me realize this is a good thing, as I'm terrified of needles or being poked or prodded in any form or fashion. It dawned on me that I hadn't had a physical in 14 years, so last Friday after work. I traipsed over to my doctor in Goldsboro to get everything checked out.

At the beginning of the examination, a nurse took my blood pressure; well, actually I still have it — she just checked it. As it turns out, my blood pressure was fine. They weighed me, and although bolts and springs didn't shoot out of the machine like I'd envisioned, it did cause me to renew my quest to lay off the corn syrup for a while.

After the nurses got through kicking the tires, I was taken back to a little room. The room was so quiet that I could hear the blood pumping through my ears. Seeing the container of used needles probably made that perfect blood pressure kick up into third gear. Just as I'd just about figured out which ceiling tile to remove and escape through, the doctor came in, so I was stuck.

The first part of his examination was a piece of cake, as it was a Q and A: "Have you been passing any blood?" "Having any trouble sleeping?" "Any strange dreams involving Dan Rather and a soap salesman?"

Next, the doctor examined my eyes, heartbeat, and, at one point, he tapped on various portions of my chest and back as if he were looking for a stud in a wall. At this point, I asked him if he was going to have to draw blood, and he replied that he did not. With that information, a wave of relief fell over me like dark on midnight.

As I was already mentally preparing what kind of skipping I'd be doing down the hall as I left his office, he told me that he needed me to drop my pants and check out the plumbing. I wasn't thrilled with this, mainly because I didn't want him to see my tattoo that sometimes read "TARHEELS', and sometimes read "THS" — it all depends on many things, including my mood

85

and whether or not that cute little number down at the utilities office is wearing that corduroy jumpsuit or not.

I dropped trou and I've gotta say I was taken aback when the doctor started checking the kiwis and asked me to cough. There was no need for him to ask, as that initial grab was the catalyst for several coughs, grunts and salutations. Thankfully, everything was fine with the faucet, but before I could make my escape, the doctor opened a drawer and removed a tube of lube.

I immediately started an internal monologue between myself and God. I was offering up close family members as sacrifices if he could get me out of this one, but alas, the big guy had better things to do and I had no choice but to turn around and assume the position.

As I grabbed that exam table and braced myself for the worst, I remembered that scene in Fletch when Chevy Chase had his transmission checked and launched into an impromptu rendition of "Moon River." Fletch was a comedy, so even though what was happening was embarrassing, surely it couldn't be all that bad, right? Right?

I heard the snap of a glove and figured the Ramrod Express was about to leave the station, but then the doctor strapped on a mining helmet and a pair of goggles. By now, the passageway the poor doctor would have to travel to get where he was going had tightened up to the point of being able to squeeze a lump of coal into a diamond. This situation made that whole "camel through the eye of a needle" deal seem plausible.

That area had puckered up so tight they called in the fire department to assist. A 23-year veteran of the fire department said he'd never seen anything a 400-pound shot of water couldn't disengage.

After the fire department left in defeat, I ended up taking a bucket of horse tranquilizers and the doctor was able to do his thing. As it was happening, a group of nurses held vigil outside the exam room and sang an a capella version of Berlin's 1985 hit "Take My Breath Away." In an attempt to add levity to the situation, right in the middle of the procedure the doctor yelled out "RICOLAAAAAAAAA!"

Although it felt like an hour, after a few seconds it was over and everything was OK, although when I turned around to get dressed I was alarmed to notice his watch and wedding band were both missing.

I left the doctor's office, but what happened at the doctor's office didn't leave me. For the rest of the night, I refused to let anyone stand behind me, which explains why it took me four hours to check out at the grocery store. Everybody thought I was being nice when I was just being cautious.

As for the doctor and me, we've decided to remain friends but to see other people.

ALL-MALE HOOTERS COMING TO AREA
MAY 20, 2010

In an effort to reshape its image, Hooters of America, Inc., has announced it will be opening a string of all-male restaurants in the southeastern United States. The first of the mammary-free wing joints is scheduled to open in Kinston in the fall.

"For years, feminists and other granola-chomping nutbars have accused us of being a sexist organization," Hooters Media Consultant John "Not Don" Johnson said. "We figured an all male Hooters would shut 'em up; I suggested we just make the current waitresses wear berkas out of spite, but I got outvoted."

The idea to say ta-ta to the Ta-Tas had many bumps in the road to overcome before it became a reality. Local newspaperman and former Mr. October in the ill-fated 1994 Gender Neutral Hooters Calendar Bryan Hanks said bringing Hooters to Kinston "was like having to ascend two fleshy gelatin-esque mountains while doing an impression of a motor boat."

"It was hard," Hanks said. "Hooters' first choice was obviously San Francisco, but having the Patrick Holmes Spandex Emporium right here in town clinched the deal."

Holmes could not be reached for comment, although he did issue the following statement through a subordinate who appeared to be malnourished and possibly beaten: "If you write about me in that column again, I will fire you."

The only roadblock to the banana hammock edition of Hooters may be the pool of qualified male wing distributors.

"Most of the applicants who've applied for work at the Kinston location are obese, have an extra belly button, or are so hairy the Brazilian waxing bill alone would bankrupt us in a week," Johnson said. "It's like some of them have Buckwheat in a headlock down there."

Local celebrity and former Howard Stern paramour Paulette Burroughs has landed a gig at the new tripod-friendly Hooters.

"I had a fresh vodka stand when I was a little girl," Paulette said. "As I squeezed the juice out of those potatoes, I dreamed of the day I could work at a place full of scantily clad men who smelled like fried chicken. For years I've had to settle for working at The Free Press where the men all wear khakis and smell like defeat."

Burroughs said her duties at the new Hooters include back-hair maintenance and mustache shellacking.

While activist Gloria Steinem has been crocheting a victory mural out of old bras and bitterness, other women see the all-male Hooters as hurting their livelihood.

"We've got children to feed and husbands to support," said Hooters' waitress Cassie Smith from her home in Michigan. "A 300-pound executive told me to lose weight or I'd lose my job. I threatened to sue, so they started this 'all-male' Hooters thing. The only downside is that now the wait staff is hitting on the customers."

LA GRANGE MAN CAUGHT STEALING
ELECTRICITY FROM KINSTON
MAY 25, 2010

Like most of you, I started dancing professionally at the age of 15. After a few years at Julliard, I toured as part of the Fruit of the Loom Follies, playing the part of the dancing apple. The tour was going great until the cops arrested us all for singing "Who Put the Poo in my Shampoo" at a fundraiser for the Sisters of Perpetual Looseness softball team.

Years later, I moved back to Lenoir County because of its proximity to the beach, its friendly people and its No. 1 ranking in Zagat's "buffets-per-resident" category. The only downside is the City of Kinston electrical rates.

Even though I live out where the buses don't run, I'm still on the City of Kinston electrical system. We have neighbors who live less than a few hundred yards away from people who are on Tri-County Electric, and even though they have the same sized houses and the same number of family members, the family that's hooked up to the City of Kinston pays much more for electricity.

Eventually, a boy from the Tri-County family married a girl from the City of Kinston family, which led to the Tri-County family allowing the City of Kinston family to run a drop cord from their house, thus saving them a couple of thousand dollars per year.

Last week while at my parent's house, I saw an old John Fogerty video with his song 'The Old Man Down the Road'. In the video, the camera follows a guitar cord over miles of roads, woods and swamps. At the end of the video, we see that the cable is hooked up to Fogerty's guitar, a leprechaun jumps out of the woods and fires a flare, and it's a happy ending.

That video got me thinking that somebody in another town might be stealing electricity from Kinston. Armed with a flashlight and half of a Twix left over from breakfast, I headed out to scour the county in search of the electrical bandit.

With my trusted dog Lucy sitting firmly on the porch and refusing to tag along, I set out on my journey. After a few hours wandering through the woods and fields near the La Grange/Kinston border, all I'd found were a couple of empty beer cans, a rusted out 1972 Impala and 27 meth labs. Just as I was about to give up, I noticed a bright orange extension cord popping up out of the ground.

For the rest of the day, I followed this orange extension cord through several communities: Fields' Station, Bucklesberry, Jenny Lind, Merle's Corner, Jed's Elbow and finally, La Grange. The cord ran behind Ken's Grill, BJ's, The Sandpiper, across U.S. 70 and into the La Grange city limits.

Whoever ran this cord took great care to weave it around every tree and pole in its path. I'd traveled at least 30 miles so far and there was no end to the cord in sight.

Just as the sun was starting to go down, I found the end of the cord. It was plugged into a detached office behind a residence, and the sounds of reggae music were blaring through open windows.

I knocked on the door, and a man by the name of Cecil Burke came to the door. Mr. Burke was wearing a pair of large Elton John-style sunglasses, a Panama Jack beach shirt, flip-flops and a bathing suit. In the back corner of the office was a running hot tub, a refrigerator full of RC Cola and Moon Pies. Next to that refrigerator was another refrigerator that was empty, but the door was left open apparently to cool the room.

When I asked Mr. Burke about this setup, he broke down and told me that years ago when he was a City of Kinston electrical customer, something horrible happened.

"I was watching UNC vs. Georgetown in the 1982 NCAA championship game," Burke said as he took a swig of RC for courage. "It was near the end of the game, and Michael Jordan was about to make the game winning shot, and my lights went out. There were no storms, no accidents, no birds perching on the lines for miles around."

Burke said the next day he ordered the 38-mile electrical cord from NASA.

"Not many people know this, but back in the old days, NASA used to run a drop cord from the Space Shuttle down to Cape Canaveral," Burke said. "Apparently, when they started letting female astronauts fly on missions, they still wanted to keep up with their stories, so they had to take a little TV with them."

He continued: "I had a cousin that used to change the oil on all of NASA's fleet so he was able to get me a deal on some extra long cord."

I then asked Mr. Burke if he felt any remorse for causing the citizens of Kinston to pay a king's ransom for their electricity.

"No," Burke said. "The whole town is full of Duke fans; serves 'em right."

And with that, Mr. Burke pushed me out of his office and slammed the door. I knocked on the door, but Mr. Burke just cranked up the Bob Marley and did what sounded like a swan dive into his hot tub.

As I walked down Mr. Burke's driveway to head home, his wife Grace just shook her head.

"I've tried to get him to stop stealing that electricity, but he takes his ballgames rather seriously," Mrs. Burke said. "One day I got so mad at him, I let all the water out of his hot tub, but he just filled it up with Moon Pies and jumped back in."

GRADUATES LEARN THAT SIMON COWELL IS SATAN
JUNE 01, 2010

If you've recently graduated from high school or college, you're probably looking forward to what has been described as 'a bright future'. Just typing that makes me giggle to the point of almost voiding my bladder.

Over the past few weeks you may have heard phrases such as 'Look to the future', 'The world is your oyster', 'One door closes, another one opens', 'You can make a difference', and my current favorite, 'You're generation faces a unique challenge'. I've decided to decode these banalities to expose their true meaning.

1)'Look to the future': What this really means is don't focus on what is currently going on, because things are in a mess. Even though the road of life is currently strewn with potholes that have been filled with dead possums, keep your chin up and don't mind the squishy thud as you head down the road of your early adult years. Sure, you're probably going to be in your late 60s by the time your student loans are paid off, but this ensures that no matter what kind of mess you make of your personal life, at least the college/university/taxidermy school that you owe money to will drop you a line every month.

2)'The world is your oyster': While the idea that the world is a mollusk that is easily cracked open to reveal valuable pearls is quaint, it's simply not true. If the world were cracked open you'd find lava – lots and lots of lava. The world is not an oyster; it is a spinning blue ball that is mostly water with a fiery lava center - kind of like a Cadbury Egg with a sandspur center.

3)'One door closes, another one opens': I've entered several buildings in my day, and never have I seen the mere closing of one door cause another door to open. What if all of the other doors are locked? What if a guy that was laid off decided to jam chewing gum and glue into the door locks? Besides being unlikely, it wouldn't be safe. Say you're running from a masked gunman and as you run into your house and slam the door, the back door pops open – he could run around the back and shoot you right in the scooch! Not much incentive to excel in life, is it?

92

4)'You can make a difference': Plenty of people have made a difference, but what percentages of those people have made a positive difference? Usually what happens, some visionary will blaze a trail, and then future generations will figure out how to make money off of it. For every cure for a fatal disease, there are 20 made up diseases that will cause you to take medicine you don't need that will in turn make you sick; for every Bill Monroe and John Lee Hooker there are 20 Ke$has and Nickelbacks just waiting to come along and smear their poisonous secretions all over it. In short, if you go to the trouble to create something brilliant, somebody will eventually come along and ruin it.

5)'Your generation faces a unique challenge': No it doesn't. Every generation of the modern era has faced the same challenge – a shrinking job market. There was a time when the safe thing to do would be to go into teaching or law enforcement – but now even those jobs are not safe from budget cuts. The way I see it, there are only two jobs that are safe in these turbulent times: Undertaker and drug dealer. If there are two things people love to do, it's take drugs and die. It doesn't matter if the economy is good or bad, there is always going to be a demand for illegal drugs, and there will always be a demand for dead person disposal. You didn't hear it from me, but I hear some state colleges will be offering a dual embalming/crystal meth/crack preparatory course in the fall of 2010. A young person looking to land a stable job and earn a good living for his family might want to check into that.

Seems bleak, doesn't it? It's not really that bad; in fact, I made it all up. Your years in college will be well spent. Everything you learn in school will be utilized in your daily life – except algebra – in real life there is no algebra.

It's a little known fact, but after graduation your world will immediately change. Water fountains will flow with hot chocolate; your pay will adequately reflect your value; dumb people won't drive you to the brink of homicide during your morning commute; all of the tax money taken from your pay will be spent responsibly, and eventually someone will peel off Simon Cowell's mask to reveal that he is indeed Satan incarnate.

For his sins, Satan/Simon will be stripped of his 'American Idol' duties and reassigned to a boil lancing clinic in Calcutta. All's well that ends well.

N.C. WOMAN LINKED TO GORE DIVORCE
JUNE 03, 2010

Apparently, the box is locked: Al and Tipper Gore are getting a divorce.

The official word from the Gore camp is that the divorce was a mutual decision and that there was no hanky panky, no shenanigans, no side action, nothing on the schnide, no skullduggery, no nuttin' — just a good ol' American divorce.

While the spin doctors and nurses are acting like nothing went on, an air conditioner repairman who worked exclusively for the Gores said Mr. Global Warming has been inhaling too many carbon credits.

"First off, Gore isn't fat — he keeps all the dough from his speaking engagements on his person," said the air conditioner repairman who asked to be referred to as Mr. Tibbs. "Secondly, Al's years with Bill Clinton were not wasted, as Bubba taught RoboBubba a thing or two about picking up women."

According to Tibbs, while on a diplomatic trip to the Orient, Clinton introduced Gore to a shaman who schooled him in the ancient ways of achieving inner peace, understanding and how to pitch a woo that was slicker than boiled okra.

"When Clinton and Gore stopped at the Kinston airport in 1992, they were served barbecue from a local restaurant," Tibbs said. "Gore took a shine to the woman who delivered the food; before the campaign stop was over, the delivery girl and Gore retired to the back of the campaign bus and they could be heard singing a filthy version of Fleetwood Mac's 'Don't Stop' until the wee hours of the morning."

That delivery girl now works as an attrition specialist for The Free Press of Kinston. Her name is Paulette Burroughs.

"I was working as a waitress at a cocktail bar," Burroughs said. "I was also working part time at Pete Smith's Laundromat and BBQ, and the Clinton/Gore campaign ordered some food and I got to deliver it."

Burroughs said her bosses — Sherry and Allison (now cable television experts) — warned her to be careful around Clinton, as it was widely known that he'd hit on more women than Rosie O'Donnell at Lilith Fair.

"I always kept a few hush puppies in my pockets for emergencies," Burroughs said. "As I was taking the food up to their bus, some barbecue and slaw spilled out of the bag and got all over my clothes.

"As I turned to leave, I could hear Gore ask an aide to 'Find the women in possession of that intoxicating odor.' The aide pulled me aside and gave me a key to Gore's room. Before I knew what was going on, Gore and I were in a deep embrace and he yelled out 'MORE COLESLAW! COOK THE HUSHPUPPY! COOK THE HUSHPUPPY!' "

Tibbs said, "Tipper started getting suspicious when she kept finding empty bottles of Texas Pete under the seat of Gore's SUV. Most of the time, Al was a normal guy, but when the lethal combination of fire-grilled pork and a sporty woman entered the mix — Katie, bar the door!"

Burroughs would not go into further detail, only to say that she and Gore did carry on a relationship for the next 15 years, and that she will reveal the full story in her new book "More Sauce Please: The Gore-y Details"

TV STAR RETURNS TO KINSTON FOR 20-YEAR REUNION
JUNE 10, 2010

Some folks have brushes with famous people; others end up eating lighter-fluid-flavored steaks with them at the beach. This weekend, a former Kinstonian who made it big in Hollywood is coming back to town for a high school reunion, and it just so happens that this person will be crashing on my couch.

The show would be called "My Name Is Paulette" and it would follow Paulette Burroughs' exploits after hitting it big on one of her monthly trips to Atlantic City. Instead of going around town righting past wrongs, though, Paulette would use her newfound wealth to belittle and demean those who wronged her in the past.

The person I'm talking about is Michael Gagliano. Mike and I met at North Lenoir High School and bonded over a disdain for book lurnin' and a love for music. I remember sitting in class and passing tapes of The Who and Deep Purple back and forth as the teacher berated a girl for daring to prop her feet on the desk of the student in front of her.

Mike was also one of the guys that helped me along when I started playing guitar. The time spent at his home crouched over a guitar were some of the best of my high school years. It was also fun eating at Mike's house, as this was my first exposure to an Italian family. It was hard to eat as I was laughing continuously at the way his parents and brother smacked each other around verbally. This may have been casual conversation to them, but to me, it was the best dinner theater I've ever seen.

I'd always thought Mike was a good friend, but I got confirmation on the evening of the one and only party I ever threw. My mama put out a great spread of food and punch, and we invited about 25 people over to the house.

Some of you may have noticed that I didn't mention the all-important word "beer" in that previous sentence. I didn't mention beer because we didn't have any. I'd warned everybody that was invited that there would be no hooch at the party, and that if they were going to whine and complain about it to please not show up.

The party went pretty well, but as I expected, a few folks started whining about the absence of beer. Not being the calm, sensible adult I am now, I expressed my feelings in a rather vulgar manner that would have caused Richard Pryor to blush.

The way I remember it, Mike — along with the Barwick brothers (Mike, Kevin and David) — tried to talk some sense into the guys who couldn't live one evening without beer, but in a way I'm glad it happened. It's always good to know who your real friends are.

Consequently, the green punch at the party made quite an impression on Mr. Gagliano. For the next week, his tongue and anything that exited his body was green. We all called him David Banner for a few days — it was fun.

Mike was a disc jockey at the LCC radio station back in the day, and I used to love helping him take requests on his Saturday night show. Usually, it would go something like this:

Caller: "Hey, this is Tammy, and I'd like to dedicate 'Nothing Compares 2 U' by Sinead O'Conner to Josh – I LOVE YEWWWWW JOSH! WHOOOOOOOOO!"

Mike (coached by me): "Thanks for that dedication, Tammy; here's your song" (cue "Ace of Spades" by Motorhead).

After school, Mike got a job at WRNS as the midnight-to-6 disc jockey. At the time, I was a table maintenance coordinator at The Beef Barn, and after work, I'd take any extras or stuff that got burned but was still edible over to the WRNS studios and we'd chow down. My hand to God, there was no silverware of any kind in their break room, so I'll leave it to your imagination as to how those extra-well done steaks got eaten, although I can tell you that it looked like a crime scene when we were finished.

After a few years of driving the WRNS boom box around Eastern North Carolina, Mike moved on to Michigan for a gig in rock radio and has been there ever since. I've visited him twice — once with our mutual friend Jode Haskins and most recently with my wife. On that last trip, Mike got us tickets to The Who/Robert Plant concert in Detroit. Seeing The Who with one of the guys that got me into them was as the kids used to say — cool.

While Mike has made a name for himself in radio, he's also done work in TV as well. In 2002, Mike played the part of "Alf" in a pilot that was supposed to be a reboot of the classic 1980s sitcom that featured a cat-eating alien. In 1993, Mike stepped in for an ailing Abe Vigoda to play the part of Norm's wife Vera on the last season of "Cheers."

Mike's biggest TV gig to date came in 2007 when he was cast in the Australian version of "The Commish". The show's producers sighted Mike's uncanny resemblance to original series star Michael Chiklis and his ability to filet a kangaroo in 45 seconds as the main reasons he got the gig.

I'm really glad Mike is in town this weekend, although I'm not looking forward to having my couch recovered on Monday.

DEPARTMENT OF JUSTICE STILL PICKING ON KINSTON
JULY 13, 2010

While sifting through a pile of arrest reports on Monday, I tried to come up with subject matter for this column. I'd written down several ideas over the weekend, but nothing seemed to catch fire.

One idea came on Saturday when I stopped at a Goldsboro gas station. After I went inside and successfully bartered what I represented as two dozen mule eggs for a gallon of gas, seven bikers pulled into the station. Along with more tattoos than an NBA potluck dinner and mufflers that were almost as loud and annoying as Joy Behar, the bikers all had beautiful women on the back of their bikes — all but one.

Always trying to keep the screen door open to the right side of my brain for column ideas, I just knew this guy would have a great story. I walked over and asked him why all of the other bikers had women with them but he didn't; he went into a CSI-level detail about the years before the "procedure" when he was known as Ginger.

Another idea that fizzled was to have the Ku Klux Klan and The New Black Panther Party settle their differences via an Ironman-type of decathlon. The activities would be filmed for a new reality show called "The Amazing Racists," as the two teams competed in events such as race-baiting, intimidation, best costumes and best parade formation.

The show would be produced by David Duke and Louis Farrakhan and hosted by Mel Gibson and Jeremiah Wright. The show already had one sponsor with a catchy slogan: XENOLD SPICE, The Deodorant for the Intolerant: "Just because you are hateful doesn't mean you have to hate the way you smell."

Sadly, the reality show got shut down by Assistant Attorney General Loretta King. She told officials from several television networks that she knew what was best for them, even though two-thirds of the people involved wanted it.

With my best ideas fizzling out and no inspiration on the horizon, the cavalry rode in via a phone call from Free Press Managing Editor and licensed massage therapist Bryan Hanks. As it turns out, Bryan was putting together a team of desk jockeys to "compete" in a charity volleyball game on Thursday night.

"I'll be glad to do it as long as everybody involved realizes that we are not playing for the NCAA Championship," I said. "Those guys who played in the United Way Day of Basketball game earlier this year acted like it was UNC/Georgetown '82; I've already tricked a good-looking woman into marrying me, so I have no one to impress."

Aside from the possibility of a game for a good cause turning into Thunderdome 2010, I haven't played volleyball since a UMYF picnic in 1988, and I wasn't exactly graceful then. Is volleyball the one where you knock it over the net, or does it involve shoving a puck across the deck of a ship with a nice retired couple from Newark?

Honest to God, I'd rather just volunteer for an hour in a dunking booth. Whoops — just received an e-mail from Loretta King at Justice Department — dunking booths have been deemed unconstitutional.

Shifting into the harsh light of reality for a moment, you've probably read that the Humphrey family of Deep Run recently lost two children in a car accident. The family is obviously going through a rough time, so South Lenoir Athletics Director Lisa Smith — along with other area volleyball coaches — have organized a charity event to aid the family.

At 7:30 p.m. Thursday, a team consisting of area volleyball coaches will take on a team consisting of Brian North and Derek Bayne from WCTI-12, Brian Bailey from WNCT-9, Billy Weaver and Brian Meador from WITN-7, with Bryan Hanks, Ryan Herman and myself representing The Free Press.

However, the doors open at 3 p.m. for a prep volleyball jamboree featuring teams from South Lenoir, North Lenoir, Swansboro and East Duplin high schools, among others, and admission is only $3 for all events. All proceeds will go toward the aid of the Humphrey family.

Also, please take time this week to help Free Press reader Jennifer Allen and Free Press staff writer David Anderson get out of jail — Muscular Dystrophy Association jail that is. Jennifer's bail is set at $2,500, so if you would like to donate, send your donation to Jennifer Allen, c/o NetworksEast.com, 1605A W. Vernon Ave., Kinston, NC 28504.

Anderson's fundraising goal is $1,000. Donate to him online at joinmda.org/MyLockup/MyHomepage/tabid/158634/Default.aspx or by mail at David Anderson, c/o The Free Press, 2103 N. Queen St., Kinston, NC 28501.

Donations will be accepted for three weeks following the lock-up date.

2010 STREET GANG CONVENTION COMING TO KINSTON
JULY 20, 2010

The gang problem in Kinston has become a real problem over the last decade. As more gangs weave their way into our society, the fear instilled by their presence has driven away citizens and businesses alike. Despite the valiant efforts of community leaders and private citizens, gangs seem to be a problem that just won't go away.

With that in mind, a local businessman has decided to turn lemons into lemonade and turn this gang problem into a moneymaker for our fair city.

"While on vacation a few years back, I visited Roswell, New Mexico," said local entrepreneur Alvin Q. Green of Jeckyl Drive, La Grange. "Some kind of aircraft crashed in the desert out there in 1947, and now folks from all over the world flock into that town looking for little green men — all the while spending their little green money."

Green says when he saw a grown man spend $30 on an ashtray shaped like a flying saucer, a switch went off in his head.

"Roswell has aliens; Kinston has gangs — makes sense to me," Green said.

The 2010 Inaugural Street Gang Convention is expected to bring close to $500,000 in revenue to Kinston over Labor Day Weekend this September.

"Gang members from all over the country will be renting hotels, dining in our restaurants and buying spray paint from our businesses," Green said. "Having the gang members in town will also help with many overdue remodeling projects, so if you're a property owner, be sure to have your insurance paid up, because most likely anything of value will be destroyed, damaged or stolen."

While most people point out that inviting every gang member in the country into Kinston could yield massive amounts of crime and disorder, Green says those people need to look at the big picture.

"The sales of home security systems will skyrocket as the convention date draws near," Green said. "The sales tax revenue from sales of spray paint alone could finance the repaving of every street in town."

While Green hopes the Street Gang Convention will become an annual event, he's experienced his share of setbacks over the years.

"I've overseen a fair amount of failed ventures," Green said somberly. "Just after graduating college, I saw a news report that said breastfeeding was on the rise, so I decided to start a company that would manufacture utensils to aid in breastfeeding — you know, tiny forks and spoons. I assumed the more you fed them, the larger they would grow."

After fielding several angry phone calls and sitting in on a few hours of remedial anatomy classes, Green realized he was taking the term "breastfeeding" too literally and shut down the whole operation.

"I still have a warehouse full of iddy-biddy straws and Velcro bibs if anyone is interested," Green said.

Green's next venture was a chain of drive-through proctology clinics.

"That almost worked," said a beaming Green. "Who among us hasn't wanted to show off our gluteus muscles at a drive thru?"

Green says a poor choice of location led to the demise of the "Stop 'N Drop Keister Clinic."

"You'd think people would have a sense of humor about a proctologist who set up shop on Old Asphalt Road," Green said.

Green said the gang convention will feature workshops, guest speakers and entertainment by a true musical legend.

"We'll have a drive-by course set up in the parking lot so that gang members can compare notes, a keynote address about projecting the proper attitude by former Limp Bizkit frontman and reformed carrot waxer Fred Durst, and a concert by southern rock legends Lynyrd Skynyrd."

When asked why Lynyrd Skynyrd was asked to perform at a street gang convention, Green said it was a practical decision.

"We figured they were the only band around that would have as many guns as the members of the audience," Green said. "We figured this way, it would at least be a fair fight."

Tickets to the convention are available by contacting Loretta King at 202-353-1555.

'THIS MESS IS STUPID'
AUGUST 10, 2010

Last week, something happened in the offices of The Free Press that shocked everyone in the building. To lay the foundation for the abomination that occurred, let me tell you about the events that led up to … The Event.

Around 9 a.m., a very nice man came in and told me that I wasn't hooked up right, but that he enjoyed my articles. About an hour later, a very nice woman came in and said she laughs so hard reading my stuff that sometimes she starts crying.

Around noon the beautiful woman I tricked into marrying me came in with our 4-month old daughter, who was smiling and cooing at everybody in sight. Life was good, if but for a few hours.

As 1 p.m. approached, I started to get nervous because things had been going well all day. The 70-year-old computers in the office were actually working properly, the 40-pound kangaroo rat that lives in the ceiling was docile and the OSHA representative that we keep tied up in the broom closet finally stopped kicking and screaming.

Whenever things are too good for too long, I get an uneasy feeling. If I get a decent royalty check from a music project or a freelance job, within hours a car, an appliance or a pet will explode, thus sucking up every dime of my "extra" money within seconds.

The boom was eventually lowered, but it didn't cost me any money, but rather a pound of flesh.

As the sun sizzled over Queen Street from the 2 o'clock position, a short man wearing a long-sleeved cotton shirt and corduroy pants that sparked when his thighs rubbed against each other came in with a box of pies he'd made for the staff. I didn't get his name but I'd heard an episode of "Gunsmoke" on the radio the night before so, for the purposes of this exercise, we'll refer to him as "Festus."

A fellow staffer told me Festus used to work for The Free Press as a manure spreader, and judging from the amount of yammering he did in the office, I'd venture to say he was also the main supplier. After talking for only 12 seconds, his generic cigarette-flavored breath had spread all over the office, propelled by a guttural death-rattle cough that would scare Keith Richards straight.

(For the Twitter generation, replace "Keith Richards" with "Lindsey Lohan." For those of you who still think Jack Paar was the best host of the Tonight Show, replace "Keith Richards" with "Rosemary Clooney.")

Festus stood at the front desk for a while and talked about the joys of retirement. Apparently Festus and his wife have been spending their golden years converting old outhouses into antique phone booths and selling them to transplanted Yankees who wanted some ironic southern kitsch in their collection.

Eventually, Free Press Managing Editor Bryan Hanks got caught up in the conversation and called me over. I went over and outstretched my hand to shake the hand of Festus only to have Festus feign a mild stroke.

This prattling twit who couldn't pass an emissions test stood their staring at me with his jaw hanging down over his Lucky Charm-stained pajama top as if someone had dug up Hitler, Jeffrey Dahmer and P. Diddy, reanimated them and sewn them into one being.

"I got nuthin' to say; I got nuthin' to say," Festus said as he walked away holding his hand in the air as if he were hoping God would reach down and pull him up out of his nightmare. "Nice to meet you, too," I said as I went back to my desk.

At this point, I was still in a good mood, and I'm not going to let a delusional old coot with the manners of a medical test mule ruin my day.

Festus goes around talking to some of his former coworkers and after what felt like an eternity, he headed towards the door. Just as he was about to waddle out to his rusted-out Le Car, Festus stopped, angled his hooves towards my desk and walked over to me. "Jon, as a person you're fine, but this mess you put in the paper is just stupid," Festus said. "It's just too out there for me."

"Thank you for telling me you think my work is stupid, Festus," I said as I looked around my desk for something in the neighborhood of a letter opener or machete. "Just for the record, Festus, I think those pies you brought in here smell like a bag of used buzzard diapers."

"Well, if you feel that way, fine," Festus neighed as he navigated the bag of protoplasm he called a body back towards the door — or as they called it back in this day — the cave opening.

Now I ask you folks, what did I do to this man who obviously has to have someone read the paper to him? Did I ask him what he thought of my column? Did I go down to the local bathhouse and criticize his technique? No, I did not. If I'd asked Festus what he thought of my work and he replied that it caused him to lose faith in humanity to the point that he'd stopped bathing, then I would have deserved his answer because I asked for it.

I asked somebody in the office if Festus acted like that when he was employed by The Free Press and they told me that he was routinely rude to customers and coworkers alike. But since he was the only man in Lenoir County who would shovel manure without a glove or a shovel — thus saving thousands in glove and shovel overhead — the company kept him on.

How Festus made it to the ripe old age of 114 with that attitude, I'll never know. Surely along the way Festus flopped his 'tude down in front of the wrong person and had his clock cleaned — or maybe not. Maybe the previous generations had a higher threshold for other people's bad behavior.

I guess having to live through a couple of wars and the cancellation of "The Facts Of Life" made our elders tougher, thus giving them the necessary constitution to put up with other peoples' utter lack of tact.

People like Festus are the most fertile, thus ensuring that one day the earth will be infested with Festuses while the people they aggravate will be forced to migrate to the moon for a day without rudeness, modified mufflers, and Eminem.

Sadly, I have no tolerance for air travel either, so I'll be forced to stay behind and become one with the Festuses. If you see me acting rude for no reason, don't take it personal, as I'm just preparing for the future.

MAN ELECTROCUTED WHILE STEALING
AIR CONDITIONER
AUGUST 17, 2010

Lamont Cranston of Old Bridge Road, La Grange, says an odd smell woke him up at 3 a.m. on Monday.

"It smelled like somebody had put a pig on the grill and forgot to turn him over," Cranston said. "I turned over to see what time it was and the clock was flashing, so I knew the 'lectricity had been out."

Cranston said he then got dressed, grabbed his pistol and started looking around the house. Once he was satisfied that nothing was wrong inside, he walked outside.

"The dog was barking at something in the bushes behind my air conditioner," Cranston said. "Turns out there was a dead man laying there with his hand stuck on my air conditioner."

The dead man on the ground was later identified as Andrew Ridgely, 45, of Grifton. While an autopsy has yet to conducted, the preliminary results indicate Crowley had been electrocuted. When Cranston was told the news, he seemed nonplussed.

"Well that makes sense," Cranston said. "I had that thing wired to zap the (censored) out of anybody who tried to steal it."

Cranston's wife Margo told The Free Press that Ridgely "had a real surprised look on his face" when they found him.

"They found his shoes on the roof of our neighbor's house a few blocks away," Margo Cranston said.

A spokesman for the Lenoir County Sheriff's Office said the incident was currently under investigation.

Cranston — a regional manager for the Safe Cracker Security Company of Duplin, Lenoir, Jones and Greene counties, said the recent rash of air conditioner thefts "gave him a mind to take some precautionary measures."

"It's easy to do," Cranston said. "You can go to any hardware store and get everything you need to electrify just about anything; an old boy over in

Jones County who's running for public office hired me to wire up around 50 of his campaign signs."

Cranston said his device — which he is marketing as "The Thug Zapper" — can be hooked up to just about anything to deter theft. Other clients have hired him to electrify safes, refrigerators, cars, and, in one case, a husband. The device features three settings: low, medium, and crispy.

"After I hooked up those signs in Jones County, a bunch of folks set up camp a few hundred yards away and monitored the area with binoculars," Cranston said. "Every time somebody tried to tear down a sign they'd make bets on whether or not the vandal would soil his or her britches; it got one ol' boy so bad it melted his fillings; when they cooled his jaw, it had welded shut."

Ridgely's family said they plan to sue Cranston for wrongful death, although the family's attorney has yet to meet with Mr. Cranston for fear that the front door is wired also. When asked if his front door was indeed wired, Cranston would only say, "Come on up to the house and we'll find out together."

Cranston advises anyone who is planning on stealing an air conditioner to take the necessary precautions beforehand to ensure they don't get electrocuted.

"The best way to make sure a unit is safe to steal is the remove the fan cover and stick your hand in there while the fan blade is moving," Cranston said. "Most people don't know that blade in there is made out of paper, so you don't have to worry about it lopping your hand off."

LENOIR COUNTY LEGEND DIES AT 102
SEPTEMBER 23, 2010

Hollace Wells, a Lenoir County native and entrepreneur, has passed away at the age of 102.

Born into a sharecropping family in La Grange in 1908, Wells came up in a time when children had to go to work at an early age. After several years of working in tobacco and tending to hogs, Wells decided he'd had enough of manual labor and decided to head north in search of opportunity.

"He never did like workin' outside all that much," said Wells' daughter, Linda Hapsburg. "Come to think of it, he didn't like workin' inside all that much either."

While Wells enjoyed the job opportunities and lax enforcement of obscenity laws in New York and Boston, his family said he never grew accustomed to the differences in southern and northern cuisine.

"He told me the first time he went into a restaurant in New York and asked for a biscuit, the waitress slapped him," Hapsburg said. "Apparently 'biscuit' was a code word in the red light district up there."

After years of struggling to make ends meet as a door-to-door door salesman and a Rockette, Wells decided he'd had enough and came back to Lenoir County.

"He got a job working over at the prison in Johnston County," said Wells' cousin, Ashley Keene. "An inmate attacked him with a sharpened banana in the yard one day, so they promoted him."

Wells was promoted to head guard, which meant he was involved with the electrocutions of the prison's most notorious inmates.

"His nickname was 'Hotplate'," Keene said.

After retiring from the prison system, Wells got into the aquaculture business.

"He was a fan of the old James Bond movies, especially the one with the man-eating piranhas," Keene said. "A friend of his had made a small fortune as a catfish farmer, so he decided to raise piranhas."

According to press clippings from this time, Wells' piranha business was a booming success. The Lenoir County Chamber of Commerce went so far as to name him Businessman of the Year in 1978.

"It was all going fine until one of our neighbors' cows got loose," Hapsburg said. "That cow eased into one of our piranha beds to cool off and them piranhas jumped all over her; she kept trying to 'moo' but she never got passed 'mmm'."

The owner of the cow subsequently sued Wells for everything he had, thus leaving him penniless.

"It was bad after the piranha farm went under," Hapsburg said. "We had to survive on piranha sandwiches for several months, and man, are they boney."

For the past decade, Wells was confined to a wheelchair due to a hip injury he suffered during his days as a Rockette. Although his movement was limited, his spirit never waned.

"He always had a twinkle in his eye and a dirty thought in his mind," Keene said. "Until we found the wrist restraints in the medical catalog, we went through about four nurses a month."

Wells' friends remember him as a gregarious soul who enjoyed everything life had to offer.

"He borrowed $12 from me in 1943 and never paid it back," said John Johnson of Jenny Lind. "That's okay, though, 'cause if he's wearing any fancy cufflinks in that coffin, they will not make it with him to the other side."

According to his obituary, Wells fathered three children, invented the hush puppy and coined the phrase, "That's what she said." Services will be held at Crowded Acres Funeral Home at 7 p.m. on Friday.

LA GRANGE WOMAN WINS
DEMOLITION DERBY WITHOUT CAR
SEPTEMBER 28, 2010

Attendees of the 2010 Lenoir County Agricultural Fair were exposed to reams of rides, foods, and ride operators that boasted a cumulative 20-year low for un-issued arrest warrants.

While it's always fun to guess which kid is going to let go with the Technicolor yawn and blow his or her groceries from the top of the Ferris wheel, for my money the best attraction is always the demolition derby — or as my benignly perverted friend Prozac calls it, "the Double D".

A side note on Prozac — he was recently attacked by a woman whom he pulled a practical joke on. She is a new mother and while breastfeeding her baby, Prozac distracted her and strategically placed a small piece of Saran Wrap in just the right spot so as to fake the baby out.

After a few minutes of trying to figure out why her usually Hoover-esque infant was all of a sudden letting seemingly gallons of milk dribble away, the mother discovered the pulverized piece of Saran Wrap and became enraged. While Prozac guffawed to the point of inadvertently voiding his bladder, the mother proceeded to strip off his clothes, diaper him, drove him out to U.S. 70, and left him to fend for himself.

Luckily, Free Press Managing Editor Bryan Hanks was driving by on his way back from a Liza Minnelli concert.

"Haven't we all found ourselves on the side of the road wearing nothing but a diaper one time or another?" Hanks asked. "How do you think I paid my way through college?"

The demolition derby can always be counted on for muddy excitement, but this year was a first in that a woman — without a vehicle — won the competition.

"I was sitting in the stands with Paulette Burroughs," said Free Press Underwriter Samantha Stanley. "She was signing autographs for $5 each when all of a sudden a glob of mud flew directly onto the Tupac Shakur T-shirt she'd owned since she roadied for him in the early 1990s."

According to the incident report, Burroughs leapt out of the stands and approached the car she believed slung the mud at her.

"She picked up a bumper that had fallen off of a car earlier in the derby," Stanley said. "She jumped on top of the car and started beating on the hood of the car like a woodpecker on speed."

There was a simple explanation for the outburst.

"Ever since they canceled 'Guiding Light,' I've had anger issues," Burroughs said.

While the security team argued over who would have to try and apprehend Burroughs, she successful dismantled and demolished not only the car that slung mud on her, but also the other four vehicles that had — by this point — been abandoned by their drivers.

Burroughs was eventually taken down by a tranquilizer dart kept on hand in case any of the animals in the petting zoo got loose.

"Back in '86 somebody fed one of the goats a six-pack of Pabst Blue Ribbon and a bag of pork rinds," said fair organizer John Johnson. "It took four security guards and the Bearded Lady to bring that thing down."

2010 DEER SEASON CANCELED
SEPTEMBER 30, 2010

Thanks to a typographicamal error in a piece of N.C. House legislation, hunters will not be allowed to legally hunt deer in 2010.

"A legislator dictated something to an intern who was paying more attention to her Twitter account than her job," said Rep. Lucas Buck of Johnston County. "The legislator was paying too much attention to the intern's skirt to read over the document before he signed off on it."

News of the hunting ban has spread quickly through the animal kingdom. Lenoir County Twix farmer Cecil Burke says deer have been destroying more of his crop than usual thanks to the new law.

"In the old days, I could string a pie pan to a tobacco stick and that would make enough noise to keep the deer out of my fields," Burke said. "Now, they yank the plate off the stick and use it to eat off of — they're brazen, I tell ya!"

Aside from smug deer flaunting their newfound freedom in the faces of farmers, hunters who have spent large sums of money on ammunition, licenses, deer urine and rifle cozies are feeling neglected, said Jones County sportsman Ranzino Smith.

"Sure, getting up at 4 a.m. to sit in a tree stand in 30-degree weather is a lot of fun," Smith said. "But without at least a chance of blasting Bambi to Timbuktu, it doesn't seem worth it."

While Santa's deer will be able to help deliver toys without having to wear bulletproof vests this year, officials in Raleigh are trying to work out a compromise.

"In Johnston County, we knew we couldn't stop prostitution," Buck said. "So we initiated a program that allowed the hookers to operate if they delivered a hot meal to a shut-in every time they went out on a service call; we named the project 'Meals-On-Heels.' "

Buck says making deer hunting illegal will not stop folks from shooting them, so he's suggesting a "Meals-On-Heels"-type solution.

"Crime is bad right now - stock market fiends, air conditioner thieves, drug dealers, politicians who raise taxes — they're like Tribbles with pistols,"

Buck said. "Let's let the hunters go after these folks to make up for the lost deer season."

Buck says if the bill goes through, we could see deer stands popping up outside meth labs, crack houses and stock exchanges before the end of October.

"If we'd have had a couple of deer hunters perched up a lamp post outside Bernie Madoff's office a few years back, it would have saved a whole lot of misery," Buck said. "I doubt the meat would have been any good though; too greasy."

20TH ANNIVERSARY SUPPER ENDS IN TRAGEDY
OCTOBER 14, 2010

This past Sept. 21 marked the 20th anniversary of the date my wife and I started dating. To commemorate this event, I thought we should go out to dinner, which we did.

The decision to dine out was not an easy one, as the wages here at The Free Press rank just below lint inspector in a Korean sweatshop. After a few weeks of collecting cans alongside U.S. 70, selling a few pints of blood, and collecting Bryan Hanks' juice payments while he was out of town, I'd assembled enough shekels to jump the Happy Meal ceiling and take my lady out to a nice restaurant.

My wife and I have been together since I was 17, and — honest to God — she could still pass for a teenager. In some sort of Benjamin Button/Mork-like fashion, she seems to look younger every year; naturally, I attribute it to being with me for 20 years.

My folks offered to keep our two chillens for us, so we were set for our night of fine dining and romance. My wife put on a dress that looked spectacular; as for me, there's really not much that can be done. I put on a sports jacket, but it's really like putting a Band-Aid on a head wound.

We get to the restaurant, and every man in the place is trying to sneak a look at the beautiful woman with me. At one point, an off-duty police officer walked over to the table and asked my wife if she was being held against her will.

"Why would you assume she was being held against her will?" I asked Sonny Crockett.

"Well, usually when I see a woman like that with a guy like you, she's either being held against their will or being paid for her services," Crockett said.

After having a buddy of his run a background check down at the station, we were then left alone to enjoy our meal — and what a meal it was. Usually, if we eat a steak, it's actually hamburger that has been shaped to look like a steak. If we want it to look like a ribeye, we stick a cap from a 2-liter drink in the upper left corner; one time we forgot it was fake and threw it to our dog, but she ate it anyway.

The food arrives, and I cut a piece of steak that's approximately the size of a butterbean. I chew this tiny piece of steak in a normal fashion and then swallow it. Approximately 20 seconds later, it was apparent that something had gone horribly, horribly wrong.

A few years back while sitting at a stoplight near the Kinstonian Restaurant, a guy driving a moving truck rear-ended me while driving approximately 45 mph. X-rays later determined the force of the crash pushed my esophagus forward, thus making swallowing interesting from time to time.

About twice a year, a piece of food would get stuck in my throat – just about where the chest and throat meet. These unfortunate episodes never lasted more than 30 seconds, so I never paid much attention to it.

Fast-forward to the anniversary supper, and I'm now in minute 15 of intermittent bouts of involuntary full-body heaves. It looks as if the alien is trying to bust out of Sigourney Weaver but for whatever reason can't quite break through.

I kept thinking each burst of spasms would be the last, as I'm determined not to let this ruin our supper. After oh, I don't know, the eighth or ninth full-body fit, we decide to pack it in and head home. Remember, this all started from a piece of food approximately the size of a butterbean — not a dry one — a regular, nasty butterbean.

I figured we'd get in the car and I'd be instantly cured, thus making our exit unnecessary, but it was not to be. About the time we were passing Walmart, I got a case of the centipedes yet again; anybody driving next to us must have thought I had a fantastic mixtape in the stereo, because you haven't seen poppin' and lockin' like that since Kool Moe Dee performed at Ronald Reagan's second inauguration.

When it was all over, this episode took around three hours to pass. I called my parents to thank them for keeping the kids and relayed what had happened. I was then given a list of relatives who — apparently like myself — were born with some strange little pocket in their throat that caused the same sort of convulsions that I'd just suffered.

With the episode over, I decided to have a little ginger ale and a peanut butter and cracker left over from my daughter's lunch box. The ginger ale went down no problem; I took a small, dainty, teeny-tiny, baby-aspirin-sized bite of the cracker, and within seconds the convulsions started again.

Two hours later, this second episode was over. My throat felt like I'd swallowed a few yards of barbed wire, and the noises that emanated from my body during the ordeal set off several security systems in the greater La Grange area.

With the realization that I'd be limited to a diet of soup and seltzer for the rest of my days, I turned to my wife and reiterated: Happy Anniversary.

CRACK EASIER TO OBTAIN THAN VEHICLE TAGS
OCTOBER 19, 2010

Last week, I had to renew the tags on my 1934 blue Chevrolet. Like the Silent Flame tobacco harvester from my youth, it's held together with bailing wire and old chewing gum, but at 198,000 miles young it gets the job done; and by job, I mean it allows me to creep in and out of Kinston five times a week.

When Ol' Blue isn't dodging gunfire on the streets of Kinston, she stays docked so as to maximize the gasolinic possibilities of the limited amounts of dinosaur juice in her belly.

Back in the 1990s, I was hoping the "Jurassic Park" movie craze would spur some egghead somewhere into regenerating a fleet of dinosaurs that could be domesticated, trained to be pets and then liquidated and placed in my gas tank. I know for a fact that the same thing could be done with cats, but due to the powerful cat lobbyists in Washington, cat-powered vehicles have gone the way of the electric car and Richard Simmons' girlfriend.

The irony of spending $28 on tags for a vehicle that is worth $25 — at most — isn't lost on me, but financial considerations aside, it's just a hassle. Usually whenever I head to the mall to renew my tags, there is a line from here to Denver, but last week I slithered in to find all windows wide open. Sensing that things were starting to turn around for old JD, I had a spring in my step as I approached the window with debit card in hand.

Before I could finish the first verse of the Katrina and The Waves hit "Walkin' on Sunshine," the lady behind the glass informed me that I had to have either cash or check — no debit or credit cards accepted. I didn't really understand this because, according to incident reports, there are drug dealers and hookers that now accept plastic, but the state of North Carolina can't.

It shouldn't be easier to buy rocks than vehicle tags, but I digress.

As I turned to crawl back out to my car I noticed some genius had placed an ATM machine on the wall. The problem is that it was one of those ATMs that charge a fee to use it, and then your bank will charge another fee, I guess because it feels as if you're cheating on your bank.

Heaven forbid you slide that worn piece of demagnetized plastic through a foreign slot; it's like divorce court on speed — a settlement is reached within seconds of straying.

Not wishing to spend upwards of $7 for the privilege of spending my own money, I walked back to the car and drove to my bank's ATM. When I walked up to the ATM, I noticed a woman with at least five receipts in her left hand and her debit card in her right hand. This led me to believe she only came down out of the mountains once per year to handle all the banking needs of her extended family.

"I swanny," said the woman. "I just can't get used to this machine."

"To be sure, not," I said in a feigning manner.

As I stood behind the lost Gabor sister while she tried to reason with the ATM by talking to it, I grew a beard, enjoyed the changing of the leaves and received my first Social Security check. After the entire region had flooded, frozen over and once again melted and receded, Eve's aunt finally finished her transaction.

"That was a lot of rigmarole just to check my balance," she said.

Finally I get the required $28 and head back to the mall to renew my tags. Of course the line is now longer than a politician's nose, so I get in line.

Person in line: "Hey, don't you write for The Free Press?

Me: "Yes, I do."

Person in line: "Why don't they put more news in there?"

Me: "You mean like the Braxton/LaRoque controversy?"

Person in line: "Oh, I must have missed that one."

Me: "Or the teen homicide suspect being arrested?"

Person in line: "Uh, I guess I missed that one."

Me: "How about the article on Chaps Restaurant?"

Person in line: "Y'all did a story on that?"

Me: "You just read the obituaries don't you? Don't you?"

Person in line: "Well, um … yeah, I reckon so."

With my tag in hand, I headed out to the parking lot only to find a truant trying to steal the license plate from my car. Just as John Travolta said in "Pulp Fiction," it was worth the little creep doing it just so I could catch him.

After sneaking up behind him and yelling an adjective in his ear that can't be printed here, young Gotti froze in his tracks.

"Oh man, you work for The Free Press?" he said, and with that, he reached in his coat pocket and handed me the wallets he'd stolen earlier that day.

"Here," he said. "You need these more than I do."

BIAS IN THE FREE PRESS RILES READERS
OCTOBER 28, 2010

I will be so glad when these elections are over, I could spit cheese grits. Between the TV ads, the flyers in the mail, the sniping online and the promised payoffs to columnists that haven't come through, this political season has turned into one giant pain in the caboose.

The latest abomination to cause needless strife around here is a political advertisement on Kinston.com, home of The Free Press online. Yes people, we are a newspaper; we sell advertising. I know that's a radical idea to some, but in these tough economic times it just doesn't make sense to give a newspaper away for free; which reminds me — Kinston.com is a free site.

If it was up to me, there would be a small monthly fee to have access to it, but since they won't even let me run the microwave — much less the paper — you're all free to continue complaining about something that you consume that you are not being charged for.

This is of particular concern to me because I spend a fair chunk of my day updating the site, promoting it, and removing reader comments that contain foul language and personal attacks, only to then answer e-mails and phone calls by the same potty-mouths who think their freedom of speech is being trampled on.

The aforementioned advertisement — for Democratic candidates — currently loads when Kinston.com opens. I was told by someone high up in our company that The Free Press also tried to sell an ad to the Republican Party, but they were not interested in buying one. Is this a case of fiscal responsibility, lack of funding, or plain old decision making? Somebody get Bob Woodward on the phone.

The Free Press DOES NOT ENDORSE CANDIDATES. I capitalized and bolded that part because some of our readers have the habit of looking at a headline, and instead of READING THE ARTICLE, they jump to a conclusion, which then turns into a widely-circulated rumor, and before you know it I've got the N.C. Wildlife Commission calling to ask why I said the 2010 deer season was canceled.

Although the thought of it makes Michael Moore's morbidly obese body shiver, for the time being, we are stuck with capitalism. For capitalism to work, businesses that provide goods and services must be paid for them. If the Committee to Invade Canada and Turn It into a Fish Camp wanted to buy an ad, we'd gladly accept their weirdo Monopoly-like money.

Another issue — on Kinston.com, we have several videos of local candidates explaining why we should vote for them. Before these videos run, commercials run. You folks have heard of commercials, right? When you're eating supper and during the national news they show a man and woman sitting in separate tubs on a cliff – those aren't short films produced by the UCLA film school, those are commercials.

One of the commercials that ran on our video section this week was for a condom company, and you'd have thought we'd beheaded Barney the Dinosaur and passed out spoons. How dare we run a commercial that has run on network TV for the past decade? Sure, families all over the country have to sit through erectile dysfunction advertisements as they split a TV dinner four ways, but surely this condom ad on Kinston.com was a calculated attempt to soil the reputation of a political candidate.

Folks, if the parents of some of these twits in Washington had used a condom, we might not be in the mess we're currently in.

This morning, a reader called and complained that an article about the local clerk of court race was biased towards one candidate. A few minutes later as I made my rounds, another person who is apparently allergic to mouthwash tried to corner me and accused us of showing bias to the OTHER candidate. How on earth can the same article be bias in two different directions? Granted, I attended ECU, but I think the basic laws of physics prohibit such an occurrence.

To all the Republicans who think we are a liberal rag intent on pushing the Democratic agenda, you are wrong. To all the Democrats who think we're a big business front for the Republican Party, well, you're wrong too. The Free Press will not be buying voters breakfast and busing them to the polls, and The Free Press will not be paying people to show up at rallies and act foolish; we'll leave that sort of thing to your beloved political parties.

DEAD BODIES TO APPEAR IN BEER COMMERCIALS
NOVEMBER 16, 2010

Last week, multiple media outlets reported the Food and Drug Administration's desire to place photos of corpses and people with holes in their throats on packages of cigarettes. As a person who is a descendant of tobacco farmers and who spent many summers scraping the black butter that is tobacco tar off of my cropping arm, this notion of labeling cigarette packages seems a bit odd.

For starters, is there anyone on the planet — from the highest building in New York City to the deepest cave in Tora Bora — who doesn't know smoking cigarettes is bad for you? Honestly people, have any of you ever met someone who started smoking because they thought the yellow film it left on their teeth would help prevent cavities?

Some people with knowledge of the subject along with a few that just look good on the TV tell us that reducing the number of smokers would help lower health care costs. A doctor at Brody School of Medicine at ECU told a WITN reporter last week the number of cancer patients admitted to their facility had tripled in recent years.

My question is this: If the number of people who smoke goes down every year, why are the occurrences of cancer going up? Could it have anything to do with the chemicals in our food or the petroleum-based products that our food is now housed in? Why don't we start putting pictures of obese people on buckets of chicken and photos of brain rot on the front of Kanye West and Taylor Swift albums?

I don't have the time, financial backing or raw tonnage of Michael Moore at my disposal, but late last Wednesday I decided to use my 15 minutes of local fame for the betterment of our society. With the help of a six-gallon bottle of Mt. Dew I stayed up all night sending e-mails to various members of the FDA, pleading with them to place shocking images on beer bottles.

With the e-mails sent, I headed to New Jersey last Thursday morning with the knowledge that I'd done my part to make the world a better place. As I sat a table at Kenny's Castaways in New York City on Saturday night, I watched hordes of people swill beer with all the gusto of a kamikaze pilot with an overdue library book. In one instance, I saw a guy's liver offer the bartender $50 to stop serving his master.

I asked the guy why he was drinking so much, and he pointed to a beautiful woman wearing a skirt shorter than the attention span of the average cable news viewer. He said he was too nervous to talk to her sober, so he was drinking to "get his courage up." The Soused Marauder finally got a snoot-full and walked over to the woman and started talking to her. Within seconds, not only had she made it clear that she didn't even acknowledge his existence, he ended up barfing up everything but his skeleton.

Another guy in the bar carried a spare liver in a red Coleman cooler. After his 10th beer, he whipped out a Ka-Bar pocket knife, yanked out the quarrelsome liver, threw it in the trash, and slapped the new liver in its place. His girlfriend pulled a needle and thread from her bustier and closed the wound. Feeling revitalized with his new liver in place, the beer hound proceeded to burp Gordon Lightfoot's "Sundown" and ordered a round for the house.

When I got home Sunday night, I was delighted to find a response from the FDA in my email. As it turns out they passed my beer bottle recommendation on to the head-knockers and — lo and behold — they've decided to convert my knee-jerk reaction into policy.

Starting in April, all beer manufacturers will be required to place pictures of diseased livers on their products. In addition to product labeling, all televised beer commercials will be required to feature no fewer than six dead bodies to represent the victims of drunk driving. It'll be real interesting to see those pristine models going to grab a brew after the beach volleyball game while having to step over the dead bodies piled around the cooler. Some genius director will probably take advantage of the rigor mortis and turn the corpses into chic beach chairs.

For whatever reason, drinking has been deemed a socially acceptable pastime, while smoking has worse P.R. than Mel Gibson in Jerusalem. I've often wondered if tobacco was a predominantly Northern phenomenon and beer manufacturing was strictly Southern, would the situation be the same. I've also wondered how many people would still be alive if Ted Kennedy and his kin were chronic smokers instead of hall of fame lushes.

For our eighth-grade trip, our class was taken to Washington, D.C., I literally bumped into a red-nosed Ted Kennedy on the steps of the Senate, and then-N.C. senator Jesse Helms took our class down onto the Senate floor. As he showed us around, I noticed Helms had a little bit of what appeared to be snuff juice on the right side of his mouth. Both men's political sins aside, which one of them would be most likely to contract lip cancer — thus hurting himself — and which one was most likely to get behind the wheel while drunk and plow into our bus as we rode back to the hotel?

I don't like cigarette smoke, and I understand people not wanting to ingest smoke that has been inside someone else's body while they are trying to eat. Additionally, I don't like loud drunks who blame their boorish behavior on being drunk as if it is a "get out of jail free" card.

As long as you aren't hurting anyone else, you can put asbestos on a cracker and eat it for all I care. America is becoming such a nanny state that twits are now living to ripe old ages; these twits vote and write policy — policies such as putting pictures of a corpse on a pack of cigarettes.

Why are they doing this? They're doing what all politicians do — looking out for their own. George W. Bush looked out for big oil; Barack Obama looks out for the unions; apparently the nimrods at the FDA are looking out for the twits, who apparently will inherit everything.

PERVERT COMMUNITY APPLAUDS
NEW AIRPORT SECURITY
NOVEMBER 23, 2010

The big story that's been splattered all over TV to divert us from real news (other than who Prince Albert of Can is marrying) is that if you want to fly commercially, you're going to be subjected to a deep tissue massage by a morbidly-obese man who may or may not have been John Gotti's driver from 1980 to 1984.

If I can't get there by car, train or boat, I don't go. Between the security hassles and my intense fear of flying through the sky in a jet-propelled metal tube, it's just not worth having to purchase a new drawer full of drawers every time I fly.

Let's face it — a few years ago, a jumbo jet was taken out by a couple of geese. I've hit geese, sheep, bears, sharks and a few people with my car, and not once did I have to crash-land in the Hudson River.

While most people are against these new security measures, a small niche of citizens who live out where the buses don't run have taken to the new measures like Kanye to crazy.

"This is the best thing to happen to me since Leonard Nimoy signed my Spock ears at ComiCon '99," said Kinston-based ne'er-do-well and Free Press Managing Editor Bryan Hanks. "I asked William Shatner to pet my Tribble one year but due to an out-of-court settlement, I can't comment on that."

Raleigh-Durham International Airport Director of Security Harry Potter says the new procedures are responsible for the surge in stand-by ticket sales.

"The other day, I saw a passenger tell the screener that he'd missed a spot and demanded that he be allowed to go through the pat-down procedure again," Potter said. "One woman keeps hiding little bottles of mouthwash on her person just so we'll have to take her to the back room for a full cavity search, or — as the woman in question calls it — the "V.I.P room.""

That passenger — Paulette Burroughs of La Grange — said she thought her days of getting groped in public were over.

"I used to roadie for Sly and The Family Stone back in the 1970s," Burroughs said. "We were on the road most of the time, but I had a little apartment in the Bronx. I used the subway to get around town, and it was great because those subway cars were crammed full of people who thought the meaning of life was written in Braille on my clothes. I used to get on the train at Flatbush Avenue and by the time we made it to midtown I'd need a cigarette; it really was the birth of speed-dating."

Security measures have also been tightened at government buildings all over the country. A source at the Lenoir County Courthouse says along with the occasional pocket knife or brass knuckles, many other questionable items have been discovered.

"They've got a box of confiscated stuff behind the metal detector," Detective John Munch said. "Just looking in the box, now we've got a half-eaten honey bun, a Richard Petty commemorative truss, a six-pack of Billy Beer, an accordion, a pair of women's underwear signed by former Gov. Jim Hunt, a VHS copy of Arsenio Hall's bar mitzvah and sportscaster Marv Albert."

Citizens all over the country are uniting to opt-out of the full-body scans that are now a part of airport security. Many pundits argue these people are protesting their loss of civil liberties, while others believe these people just want somebody to play "Find The Quarter" with them.

"If you go to a strip club, it'll cost you at least $200, and you're not allowed to touch the girls," Hanks said. "These security people at the airport will get fired if they DON'T touch you, and it's FREE! This is a great country – GIGGITY!"

When asked by the Associated Press how he felt about his terrorist regime being responsible for Americans getting their freak on, Osama Bin Laden could not be reached for comment.

"He's in Los Angeles filming 'Jihad 'er Done' with Larry The Cable Guy," said Bin Laden's publicist. "We'd also like to take this opportunity to quell the rumors that Bin Laden was arrested at The Viper Room in L.A. for taking indecent liberties with a turban over the weekend."

'TWAS THE NIGHT BEFORE CHRISTMAS ... IN KINSTON
NOVEMBER 30, 2010

Usually, whenever somebody decides to improve on something that already works fine, the results can be disastrous: New Coke; pink John Deere hats; gravy flavored Crest. Other times the original can be improved on: Peanut M&Ms; Doctor Who; Cher.

This little ditty originally appeared here Dec. 11, 2008. Since my home has been turned into a MASH unit — and I am in a Nyquil-induced state of altered consciousness — I present an updated version of "'Twas the night before Christmas ... in Kinston:"

'Twas the night before Christmas, when all throughout Kinston
The wallets were starving from the money gone missing.
The credit cards were maxed-out with nary a care
In hopes that St. Ed McMahon soon would be there.
The children were nestled all snug in their beds
While their parents scratched lottery tickets till their fingers bled.
And Mama in her bathrobe, and I in my chaps
Had just settled down for a long winter's nap.
When out on the lawn there arose such a clatter
I searched through the house for a ball peen hammer.
Away to the window I flew like a flash
Flung open the door and hid all my cash.
The moon on the driveway of a midnight frost
Gave the luster of an oil leak from an oil pan of rust.
When, what to my crustated eyes should appear
But a repo man, with reposessin' gear.
With a scary old scalp, so slimy and slick
Surely he came for my treasured Crown Vic.
More rabid than badgers the payments were due
With each payment, I wrote such a note:
"I don't have it all, but I'll get it soon!"
"My workman's comp case will surely balloon!"

124

To the top of the porch I sang with my all:
"Now go away! Go away! Go away all!"
But with a set of keys from the dealership on his finger
He drove off into the night, he did not linger.
As I cried in my hands, and was turning around
Down the chimney, St. Holmes came with a bound.
He was dressed in red spandex, from his head to his foot
His nametag read "Patrick," all covered in soot.
He summoned me closer, to ask me a question
"Do you have any Tums? I've got indigestion."
With a cure in his tummy, he walked out of sight
With to my chagrin, my kiddy's new bike.
If that weren't enough to steal our elation
On the door was a notice about annexation.
The council decided our land should be theirs
Which meant our taxes would climb like the stairs.
"It's time to move," daddy said with a holler
"These people won't rest till they have every dollar!"

POOL CONSTRUCTION AT COURTHOUSE ON SCHEDULE
DECEMBER 07, 2010

If you're like me and you've had to post bail for a loved one over the past few weeks, you may have noticed the gaping hole behind the Lenoir County Courthouse.

"It's surreal to look out the back door and realize that by next summer there will be an Olympic-sized swimming pool where the parking lot used to be," Deputy Randy Holland said. "A couple of the current inmates have already started talking about forming a synchronized swim team."

Although the main purpose of the swimming pool is to create a recreation center for jailed inmates, during the winter months the pool will house the replica of the CSS Neuse that currently resides on Herritage Street. According to top secret documents obtained from the Wikileaks website, Kinston city officials plan to hold Civil War reenactments to celebrate the history of the legendary boat.

"We're hoping the noise caused by the battle reenactments will drown out the gunfire from the drive-by shootings," said a Lenoir County commissioner who wished to remain ambidextrous. "This giant cement pond should also boost our chances of bringing the 2008 Summer Olympics to Kinston."

"Court cases can bring out the worst in people," said Judge Claire Huxtable. "If two plaintiffs are arguing over a damaged set of Richard Petty commemorative plates or a ripped Amour hair extension, I believe having them take a quick dip in the pool will help quell those disruptive tempers; if that doesn't work, there's always New Coke or Jell-o."

Downtown merchants and practioners of the apocalypse believe the courthouse swimming pool will help Kinston retrieve some of the town's kitsch value that was lost during the Toilet Paper Panic of 1954.

"That was a bad year for shaking hands," said local historian Ron Burgundy. "The cholera was so bad that year it killed off the flu, but the year off caused it to come back in 1955 with a vengeance. The flu was so bad in '55 it killed two oak trees and one Buick."

According to the Wikileaks documents, Kinston city officials believe the courthouse swimming pool will restore Kinston to the days when tobacco was king, DuPont was queen and sandwiches could be rented by the hour.

"The pool should be ready by the end of January," said Martha Westbrook of Eventually Construction Company. "Since it'll be too cold to swim, we'll be filling the pool with fish stew, which will be sold to raise money for PETA."

NEW FRANCHISE TO REPLACE KINSTON INDIANS IN 2012
DECEMBER 21, 2010

While the revelation that the Kinston Indians will be leaving town after the 2011 season is still sinking into the consciousness of the community, it appears that another professional sports juggernaut is chomping at the bit to fill the imminent void.

"It has taken years for our sport to gain the recognition it deserves," Don Clayton Jr. of the Professional Putters Association said. "Putt Putt is not just a game for children or awkward first dates; professional players such as Rainey Statum and Mike Baldoza routinely win cash prizes upwards of $25 per match."

Clayton said the PPA plans to broaden its reach by forming a series of teams that will compete on a regional level, and that Kinston is definitely on their radar.

"We realize that it could take decades to build up the kind of rapport with the public that the Kinston Indians have," Clayton said. "Half the fun of attending a ball game is getting loaded on beer and yelling at the players; we can't really have that when legends such as Danny Mac are trying to putt around a windmill."

Prozac Mills, a local alcoholic/baseball fan has been yelling drunkenly at Kinston Indians games since he was 21-years-old.

"There's two things I hate — sobriety and Putt Putt," Mills said from his room at the Gerald Ford Center in Jones County. "I used to love to get loaded on cheap hooch and criticize athletes that were doing things I couldn't do if I had help, but Putt Putt? Shoot, I've played Putt Putt drunk dozens of times — that's how I ended up with Fuzzy Zoeller's pants after the 1984 Masters."

Clayton says several investors have made verbal commitments to support what he hopes will become the Kinston Putz Professional Golf Team.

"We plan on making it cool to be a Putz," Clayton said. "Putt Putt megastar Greg Newport has agreed to scoot out the first ball on opening night, and teen Putt Putt sensation Olivia Prokopova will be handing out free putter coozies to the first 100 fans to enter the stadium."

While Kinston has produced its fair share of stellar athletes, such as Jerry Stackhouse and Reggie BUHlock (formerly Bullock), Clayton believes if Putt Putt catches on, that list could grow exponentially.

"To be honest, I don't know what exponentially means — I attended ECU," Clayton said. "But I believe there could be some untapped Putt Putt talent waiting to be discovered or woken up here in Kinston."

For more information on Professional Putt Putt, visit www.thepmga.com.

LOCAL WEATHERMEN SUFFER ON-AIR BREAKDOWNS
DECEMBER 28, 2010

Christmas is a time best analzyed after a few days of reflection, so for now we'll let that one simmer. For today's scripture, I'd like to talk about the mental breakdown of three local weathermen.

Those of you who live in dwelling with windows may have already sussed this out, but it snowed on Sunday. This wasn't the usual "looks-like-somebody-busted-an-aspirin-and-spread-it-around-the-yard dusting" we usually get in N.C.; this was a full blown "buy-a-loaf-of-bread-and-a-flat-of-vienna-sausages-and-bust-up-the-furniture-and-burn-it-for-warmth" real life snow storm.

I'm sure someone is sitting in a newsroom reading this and about to bust a vein because I refuse to use the term "meteorologist"; I will only refer to them as meteorologists when they refer to me as a linguisticist. I will also accept Experto de Wordo, The Sultan of Syllables or the Bionic Ebonic.

To their credit, WCTI's Skip Waters, WNCT's David Sawyer and WITN's Marvin Daugherty warned us all week that the snow was a-comin', and with that they polished off their Dopplers and prepared for a 48-hour non-stop overstatement of the obvious. When the snow arrived all each man had to do was look into the camera and say, "I told you so; back to you, Chet."

I understand the need for ratings, as TV stations have not been immune to the economic downfall we're all mired in. Heck, a while back WNCT fired Phillip Williams, a 20-year veteran weatherman who now blogs about weather at www.pittcountylife.com. Just so you know, I make no commission if you visit www.pittcountylife.com, but if Mr. Williams could find it in his heart to throw a brother a nickel, it would be much appreciated.

A simple weather update at the top of the hour would have been more than sufficient, but Marvin, David and Skip decided to bust a pinata with a bazooka. I was not glued to the tube this past weekend, but here is a breakdown of the incidents I witnessed from just a few minutes viewing:

Skip Waters — There was no need for Skip Waters to send an intern into the parking lot to count the snowflakes as they hit the ground, examine them and produce sketches of the different designs for the viewers at home.

Marvin Daugherty — Around hour 28 of his coverage, Marvin Daugherty looked into the camera and told the viewers they couldn't fill the empty void in their souls by watching a grown man explain to them how ice on roads and bridges is a bad thing. "I am the Lizard King," Marvin said. "I can do anything."

David Sawyer — David spent most of the time separating himself from accusations of his involvement with the Weather Underground. At 4 a.m. on Sunday, WNCT weatherman Gannon Medwick could be heard off-camera asking fellow weatherwoman Kweilyn Murphy why she wouldn't return his phone calls.

It's going to be a long winter.

SATAN DENIES TIES TO ELECTRICITIES
JANUARY 20, 2011

As I write this (on Jan. 18), today marks the 38th time the earth has circled the sun since I was assigned to earth. I was planning on writing about the festivals and ceremonial sacrifices that occurred to celebrate another year of respiration, but after opening my electric bill, I've decided to put off the birthday column until a time when I'm not ready to ask thousands of people to pay their light bills with Skittles.

Anybody that reads this column on a regular basis knows that when the Good Lord was passing out brain power, he handed me a set of Dollar Tree batteries; but, could somebody in the know explain to me why ElectriCitites customers are paying (censored)-near TWICE as much for electricity as almost the rest of the universe?

It irritates me when something doesn't make sense. Like most good Americans, when I don't have the facts, I tend to come up with my own theories and state them as fact. Here are a few possibilities I came up with:

The New Math — ElectriCities may be using that new-fangled metric system that Jimmy Carter was so Viagra-ed up for back in the 1970s. As far as we know, a "3" to us may be a "6" to them.

Typos — The person in charge of billing may be making a typo. I would imagine the turnover rate at a company with a popularity rating below that of Enron and British Petroleum combined would be constantly having to train new staff to cover the vacancies left by former employees who left to work in more desirable jobs, such as Fidel Castro's cigar tester and head of artificial insemination at the National Institute for Maggot Technologies.

Satanic Influence — Last week I wrote a column that some believe insinuated ElectriCities top brass consisted mainly of agents of Satan. While no one from ElectriCities has called, e-mailed or written a message in goat's blood on the front door of The Free Press, I did receive the following letter from Old Legba himself this week:

"Mr. Dawson: It has come to my attention that there is a rumor going around that representatives from my organization are somehow affiliated with ElectriCities.

"While we have many associates infiltrating corporations on a daily basis, even we at Helping Evil Live Longer, LLC (H.E.L.L.) have our limits. Sure, we usually jump at the chance to cause pain and suffering, but like you, we have been paying ElectriCities too much for electricity for years.

"A few years back we switched over from gas-powered flames to electric ovens because we thought it would be cheaper and would cut down on our cleanup time, but the bill we just received for December made my horns curl.

"I realize under the law you have the right to satirize without fear of prosecution, but unless you refrain from linking me to ElectriCities, I will be forced to retaliate by allowing Bon Jovi to release another album.

"The choice is yours,

Satan

(Dictated but not read)"

THE CRUELTY OF FAMILY
JANUARY 25, 2011

I'm blessed with a good family. If I were to ever need money for bail, I'm 65 percent sure they'd be right there within a few days to help me out.

That being said, within the most loving families, a certain amount of cruelty is to be expected. For example, everybody remembers that episode of "The Andy Griffith Show" where Opie bit into a cold piece of fried chicken and hit Aunt Bee over the head with a bottle of Ripple. Even beloved TV dad Bill Cosby once went crazy and tried to strangle Theo with a multi-colored sweater.

Back in the late 1950s, my uncles William and Wiley were playing under a tractor shelter. During the course of their rampage, they got into a bucket of tractor grease. Like the first caveman that discovered fire, these two truants reveled in their discovery and proceeded to sling, smear and gom that tractor grease all over each other. Then at some point they ended up on the ground wrestling — neither of them won.

Once they'd wrestled themselves tired, they walked out of the tractor shelter to find their long-suffering mother Lousie. About this time, my great-grandfather Jake drove up. He looked at William and Wiley — covered in tractor grease and mud — and then looked at my grandma.

"You know, Lousie," Jake said. "It would be less trouble to get two more young'uns than to clean those two up."

On the other side of the family and about a decade later, my cousin Gene tells the story of the time his car broke down about seven miles from home in the middle of the night. He went to a house and called home to get a ride. His father told his brother David that Gene was broke down and to go pick him up.

Ever the good brother, David rolled back over and went back to sleep — causing Gene to have to walk seven miles home in the middle of the night.

The following months went by without incident, until one night when Gene was coming in at 1 a.m. from The Hot Foot Club. He crept into his bedroom and accidentally bumped into a table which woke up his brother David.

"Why are you up?" David said in his sleepy stupor.

All of a sudden, a chance at revenge presented itself.

"It's time to go put in tobacco," Gene said. "You better hurry up so daddy doesn't have to wait; I'm going to brush my teeth and I'll be right out."

Not wanting to make everybody late, David jumped up, got dressed and went outside to wait for his daddy and brother in the truck. For his part, Gene got into a warm bed and slept until 5 a.m. — the actual time they were supposed to get up to go to work.

Gene and his daddy went outside to find David curled up in the fetal position, leaning against the dusty window of the truck. The windows were completely fogged up from the inside, with the only way to see inside being a multi-inch trail of Nab/Pepsi stained drool that covered about half of the window and was dripping out of the floorboard.

Gene opened the door and David fell out of the truck face-first into the dewy grass, although his fall was cushioned by the art project left by their beloved blood hound Jasper just a few minutes earlier.

N.C. MAN TARGETED BY ORGAN THIEVES
FEBRUARY 01, 2011

Last Thursday morning I crawled onto an Amtrak train which proceeded to hurdle blindly into that snow-bound oasis that is New Jersey. Did I mention it was cold up there? It was so cold that when House of Vibes Recording Studio mascot Buster the Dog was doing his business in a nearby park, before his master could scoop up said business in a plastic bag, it froze and slid down the street.

Eventually, the frozen poo was pulled over by a N.J. state trooper. According to the ticket, the poo was clocked going 69 mph in a 55 mph zone.

While in New Jersey, I did a bit of work on a new Third of Never (thirdofnever.com) album which should be released in the fall. While working on the music was fun, getting home was a bit of a challenge. Between navigating the schedules of a five-piece band and the whims of an Amtrak scheduler, who apparently drinks engine coolant for breakfast, I was left with very few options when it came to getting home on Saturday.

I can hear some of you thinking, "Why don't you just fly?" My response to that could be best represented in a list:

1. I don't like to fly.

2. I don't like to de-shoe in the company of strangers.

3. I don't like being frisked by a guy who sold a pint of his own blood that morning to buy meth.

4. I don't like being frisked by a guy who sold a pint of someone else's blood that morning to buy meth.

5. If the train breaks down, we just sit still; if the plane breaks down, we plummet to the earth in a screaming, bowel-voiding fireball.

6. A plane can be brought down by a flock of geese; I've seen a train wipe out an entire marching band and keep on rollin'.

Usually, there is an option to leave New Jersey at 10 a.m. on Sundays, but for whatever reason this time, my only option was to leave at 7 a.m., which meant I had to grab a transit train in Highland Park at 1:30 a.m. to catch the Amtrak train bound for Wilson.

At 2:16 a.m., I got off the transit train and plopped down on a bench next to a small police station in the middle of the Trenton, N.J., transit center. It made me feel better to know I could endure my five-hour wait in the presence of a police officer, because as we all know only unstable lunatics inhabit train stations in the middle of the night. If one of these nut jobs were going to harvest my organs to sell on eBay, then they'd have to get through Officer Vincenzo DeNunzio first.

I'd been awake since 10 a.m. the previous day, and although I'd tried to grab a little sleep at various points, there was a little too much going on. It was probably a good idea that I couldn't sleep, because every time the cop would leave the desk to make his rounds, I'd shift around on the bench to make it harder to get at my kidneys with a scalpel.

About 3 a.m., the sleep deprivation started to take its toll. I started to wander around the station and noticed that, for a train station, they had some really interesting stores. They had a book store, a pizza parlor and, the most interesting, a pie shop opened by a couple of retired math professors. Their constant special was a slice of pie for $3.14159265.

By 4 a.m., the lack of sleep was becoming a real problem. While it may have been a simple hallucination, I could have sworn Matt Lauer tried to sell me a thimble containing his remaining journalistic integrity. He only wanted $5, but since it was only half full, I had to pass.

Thankfully, Train 89 — The Palmetto — was on time, and at 7:06 a.m. that sweet, sweet "all aboard" call blasted out of an intercom system that hasn't worked properly since Jimmy Carter was in office.

As I headed for the elevator that would take me down to the train platform, I thought back over the bizarre evening I'd had. Something about the sun that was slowly creeping over the horizon gave me a second wind and I began to think a little clearer. I even laughed to myself at some of the crazy thoughts that ran through my head the night before. I mean, how could Matt Lauer have tried to sell me his journalistic integrity? He doesn't have any journalistic integrity.

The "organ thief" theory may have been off base too, but I did see a guy grasp his midsection in pain as he called his wife to remind her to pick up some liver at the grocery store.

AN UPDATE ON THE CONDITION OF BRYAN HANKS
FEBRUARY 03, 2011

As many of you know, our managing editor and sports fanatic Bryan Hanks has been out due to a medical condition.

Bryan had been in pain for several months, and after several false diagnoses, which included among other things rickets and demonic possession, the doctors discovered Hanks was suffering from a herniated disc.

I've heard about herniated discs all my life, but have never known exactly what they were. The following description was taken from WebMd.com:

"The bones (vertebrae) that form the spine in your back are cushioned by small, spongy discs. When these discs are healthy, they act as shock absorbers for the spine and keep the spine flexible. But when a disc is damaged, it may bulge or break open. This is called a herniated disc."

Until Hanks' hospitalization, I was unaware of "bad discs," other than those released by Kanye West and Taylor Swift. The doctors are unsure what caused the damage to Hanks' disc, but they are reasonably sure it has something to do with his former career as a stunt double for Paris Hilton's home movies.

Last week, doctors performed surgery to alleviate the pressure and hopefully remove the pain that has been plaguing him for close to a year now. According to the doctors, Hanks came through the surgery with flying colors, although they were a bit concerned that he kept floating in and out of consciousness and murmuring something about a tunnel, a bright light and Paul Lynde.

Since being released from the hospital, I've spoken to Hanks on several occasions. Tina — his devoted and apparently legally blind better half — has been taking good care of him. She even upgraded her cable package so he'd have plenty of sports to watch — basketball, hockey, football, tennis, boxing, donkey checkers, underwater margerine sculpture and obese luge.

What I'm about to say I'm sure will be disregarded as mere piffle, but as God as my witness on Tuesday I heard a sober, unmedicated and only mildly dispeptic Bryan Hanks say the following: "I'm tired of watching sports."

After I picked the phone up off the floor and taped it back together, I asked him to repeat himself.

"I'm tired of watching sports," Hanks said.

Obviously the man was sick, so I didn't press the matter any further. I decided then and there that I'd go into the office to clean out his desk, as obviously the doctors slipped and cut a main cable to his brain while they were working on his back.

The first thing that strikes you when you open the door to Bryan's office is the bright, Carolina blue that shimmers off of all the UNC trinkets on his desk, on the shelves and on the walls. A poster of the 1982 Tarheels signed by Dean Smith hangs next to a framed wad of gum reportedly chewed by former UNC forward Dave Popson after one of the team's many victories over the University of Virginia.

Sadly, the inflatabe UNC Tarheel chair behind Bryan's desk was in desperate need of revivement, but everybody was afraid of catching Hanks cooties, so Nancy Saunders — the person who's been steering the ship in Bryan's absence — put the chair out of it's misery with the swift stab of an ink pen. The slightly comical noise made as remaining air escaped the chair brought a tear to many of us, as it was the sort of noise that used to come from that office on a daily basis.

With the office cleaned out and the boxes of UNC memorabilia mailed to the Universtiy of Virginia's Department of Humiliation, we all lit a candle to remember Bryan Hanks — and to dissipate the smell.

GRANDMA ATE CHEETOS WITH A FORK
FEBRUARY 08, 2011

The following statement is A) true and B) never been said out loud or written by any human being on this earth or any other: My grandma used to eat Cheetos with a fork.

In her later years, grandma's taste buds gave up the ghost a bit, so finding something flavorful enough that she could taste and enjoy was sometimes challenging. If any of us saw a snack or a drink with a stronger than usual taste, we'd pick it up in the hopes that we'd found THE flavor that would get the job done.

Sometimes she'd see an advertisement for something new and ask me to get it for her, like the time she saw an ad for Pringles that boasted BOLD FLAVOR. I can't remember what the flavor was, but I remember going into every grocery store between here and the coast looking for them. Finally one day I found them, and I figured this must be what Indiana Jones felt like when he found some treasured artifact like a board from Noah's Arc or Dolly Parton's training bra.

I was so full of myself when I found those chips that I called all my relatives as if to announce the birth of a child. The last time I'd done something that filled me with that much pride is when I figured out how to change the clock on the car radio.

Dutifully I presented grandma with the chips, and after filling her cup to at least an inch over the top with ice so that the rest of the cup could hold maybe an eye-dropper's worth of Pepsi, she picked up a chip by the edge as if it were a photograph and took a bite. A few seconds passed and she put the lid back on the tube and handed them back.

"I appreciate you getting them for me," she said. "I'll let you have the rest."

The chips — like most of my efforts — didn't really make it. One day I brought her some Sedgefield pimento cheese on a whim and she loved it. "This tastes like the kind I used to make myself," she said. "We have a winner."

Although switching from the Star brand that had been in the rotation for decades was like asking a Ford man to try a Chevy, the transition of power was relatively smooth and without incident.

With that little victory, I retired from the investigative food game. Eventually, someone else in the family brought her a bag of Cheetos (the crunchy kind, because quite frankly we all know the puffy ones are just a waste of time).

As it turns out, the Cheetos did the trick, although they did present a problem: How would the cleanest woman west of the Rio Grande be able to enjoy a snack that was as messy as Cheetos?

That little thing I mentioned earlier about holding the chip as if it were a photograph was no joke; if grandma and granddaddy went to a restaurant to eat anything that would require skin to food contact, such as fried chicken, grandma would have a damp wash cloth in a plastic bag in her purse to be sure her hands didn't get gommed up.

For a while it was routine to walk into grandma's kitchen to find her eating a Cheeto, wiping the Cheeto dust off of her hand with a wash cloth while she chewed, and then repeating the process. The constant repetition of the Cheeto/chew/wash cloth motion strengthened her right arm to the point where she was able to compete in the Collective of Lady Arm Wrestlers U.S.A. (CLAW-U.S.A.). She made it to the finals in Nevada one year; she used the trophy to re-pot geraniums for years.

Eventually, grandma got tired of the big production it took to enjoy her Cheetos, and being the grandmother of invention, I walked in one day to find her eating the Cheetos with a fork. At first I didn't say anything, and after a while she looked at me with a grin and asked, "You don't think the fool catcher is going to come after me, do you?"

I told her she could eat Cheetos with a tire iron if she wanted to — whatever made her happy.

"A tire iron, Jon?" she said. "That's just foolishness."

LARRY DREW II BREAKS HIS SILENCE
FEBRUARY 10, 2011

Last week UNC basketball … uh … "star" Larry Adios Drew II skipped town in the middle of the night.

Up until a few weeks ago, Drew was a starter for the Tar Heels, but after a few years of Ann Heche-like behavior and a whoopin' by Georgia Tech that Ajax couldn't wipe off, Drew lost his starting position to freshman Kendall Marshall.

At first, it seemed Drew's demotion was a good idea; Marshall was performing well and Drew's performance improved as well. Who knows — if Drew's improvements were consistent, he may have even gotten his old starting position back. Sadly, we'll never know how that would have panned out because he pooched his lip out and ran out of town with his Huggies in a wad.

My daughter and I were in Chapel Hill last Saturday. As we made our way down Franklin Street, I showed my daughter UNC's campus on our left. The campus looked great, but the sight of Drew sneaking back on campus to retrieve a box of diapers he left in his dorm was just off-putting. Just imagine a grown man running across campus with a case of adult-size diapers — all this while sucking on his thumb and a pacifier at the same time.

I had my press badge in my coat pocket, so I walked over to Mr. Midnight Houdini and asked him for an interview. At first I couldn't understand him because his head was lodged firmly up his backside, but after a passing janitor loaned me his plunger, I helped him dislodge his noggin from his bottom with a resounding thwack.

"I would like to tell my side of the story," Drew said. "I think I've been treated unfairly in the press."

As we walked down Franklin Street, I asked Drew why he would leave the team midseason and lose credit for the classes he'd been attending.

"My father is an NBA coach," Drew said. "By proxy, that makes me an NBA player, and I thought it was disrespectful of Coach Williams to take me out of the starting lineup."

142

When I pointed out that his replacement Kendall Marshall had been thriving in the position, Drew played that off to a biased press.

"The press hasn't liked me since I got here," Drew said. "Just after I arrived in town as a freshman I went to Southpoint mall to buy some clothes, and the escalator I was riding up to the second floor of Victoria's Secret broke down. I was stuck on that escalator for over six hours, but all the local newspapers did was poke fun at me."

A few minutes into our walk, legendary UNC radio man Woody Durham walked out of a restaurant. Being a longtime Durham fan, I walked up to get an autograph, but after seeing Drew, Durham flew into a rage and began pelting both of us with a series of sharpened pennies he apparently keeps in his sports jackets for emergencies.

After chasing us up and down Franklin Street for about half an hour, four UNC campus police officers and one member of the wrestling team were able to subdue the veteran sportscaster.

"If I ever see you in Chapel Hill again I'll kick your (censored) from here to California myself — NO BATHROOM BREAKS!" Durham said as he was placed into the back of a police car.

Seconds later, a flash of bright light shone blindingly over downtown Chapel Hill and an angel holding a sword appeared in the clouds. Without saying a word, Drew walked into a nearby field and eventually out of our site.

Looking for some type of explanation, I walked into a bookstore and opened a Bible. After a bit of searching, I found what I was looking for in the Book of Numbers:

"And the ass saw the angel of the Lord standing in the way, and his sword drawn in his hand: and the ass turned aside out of the way, and went into the field."

DUKE TO FORFEIT ACC CHAMPIONSHIP
MARCH 15, 2011

As Mike Krzyzewski hugged his players after their victory over the UNC Tar Heels on Sunday, he had no way of knowing the celebration would be cut short on a technicality.

"It's the NCAA equivalent of ripping the tag off of a mattress," said Richard Clark of the Naismith Center. "After reviewing the team manager's records, it appears the change over to daylight savings time caused Duke to accidentally practice longer than they were supposed to."

What Clark is referring to is the little known section four, title 19, subsection 4.3A rule that states a team "is only allowed to practice up to two hours before game time." According to the 2010-11 edition of the NCAA manual, failing to adhere to this rule will result in "forfeiture of the game in question."

After what was described as a "robust meeting" between Krzyzewski, Clark and other NCAA officials, the Duke coach emerged from the meeting looking frazzled.

"I'll be making a statement on Wednesday," Krzyzewski said — through one of his assistant coaches.

Former sports commentator and current "Preparation H" test module Billy Packer weighed in on the controversial ruling on Monday.

"As I've been saying for years, I know more about basketball than anyone else around," Packer said. "I've been trying to tell the NCAA for years that there should be four baskets on the floor, a mud pit filled with alligators, and an electrified free throw line."

When asked to comment specifically on the Duke practice rule violation, Packer disappeared up his own backside and started to recite his lines from a 1992 "Mr. Cash" commercial.

"Duke's forfeiture means the UNC Tar Heels are now the 2011 ACC Champions," Clark said. "It also means that all of the dancing and posturing displayed on the Duke bench by Kyrie Irving cannot be used for his 'Dancing with the Stars' audition tape."

"It's a shame that Kyrie's dancing was all for nothing," said Duke basketball historian Tina Hughes. "Christian Laetner could 'cabbage patch' with the best of them, but Kyrie was throwing in bits of tap, jazz and even a few square dancing moves; he can do it all."

Due to the forfeiture, Duke will lose their No. 1 seed in the NCAA Tournament Western Division.

"Duke will be rerouted to Guam, where they'll be a No. 2 seed," Clark said. "They take on 16th seed Joe Pesci Community College Thursday at 9 p.m."

Thankful residents of the desolate island are looking forward to Duke's arrival.

"It's gets lonely out here sometimes," said former UNC guard and current director of senior activities at the Cheerful Reaper Retirement Community, Larry Drew II. "I would have left secretly in the middle of the night by now, but the next boat doesn't come in from the mainland until April."

JIMMY CARTER BRINGING
METRIC BURGER TO LA GRANGE
MARCH 22, 2011

A routine land permit check by The Free Press revealed that former United States President Jimmy Carter has purchased land in La Grange.

While a call to The Carter Foundation in Atlanta was not returned, the Free Press has learned that Carter plans to use the land to launch a string of fast-food restaurants that will promote the metric system.

"One of Jimmy's great disappointments as president was his inability to get America to switch to the metric system," said La Grange insurance agent Jon Hughes, who is also Carter's fourth cousin by marriage. "At the last family reunion I heard he and Rosalynn were going to start something called "Habitat For Hamburgers.""

A hobo who identified himself as Shelley Long told The Free Press he'd been hired by "Habitat For Hamburgers" as a short order cook.

"There ain't no 'Quarter Pounders,' " Long said. "They've got something called a '.11 Kilogrammer' and instead of the Hamburglar stealing burgers, they've got the Calculaburglar running around correcting everybody's math."

According to Rhea Pearlman at the Creative Artists Agency, the voice of the "Kilogrammer-munching mathematician" will be played by Kelsey Grammar, who himself was named after the tensor metric theory, which is Latin for "pompous center of attention."

While "Habitat For Hamburgers" will in many respects have much in common with other fast food restaurants, Long said each franchise will feature items that will hopefully ingratiate the business to the surrounding community.

"For example we've got several sandwiches named after local celebrities," Long said. "For Paulette Burroughs we've got 'The Paulette,' which consists of a hamburger patty topped with scallions, Tegretol, Colt .45 and tomato. We've also got something called 'The Annexation,' which starts out as a bacon cheeseburger, but if you end up making a mess of it you can just grab the burger of someone sitting next to you whether they want you to or not."

While many applaud the Nobel Prize Winner for Papier-Mache's efforts to get Amercia off poundology and onto the metric system, others believe it is a waste of time.

"Americans don't like change," said Ted Danson of the Jalen Rose Institute for Ignorance in Michigan. "Besides, 'pound' is a macho word; 'kilogram' sounds like somebody's trying to murder a graham cracker."

While the "Habitat For Hamburgers" restaurant chain is still in the planning stages, the organization has already offered NASCAR star Kyle Busch $1 million to drive a peanut-oil powered car for the 2011/2012 season.

"Hopefully this time next year Kyle Busch will be driving the 'Habitat For Hamburgers' car in the Daytona 500," said NASCAR Chairman Norm Peterson. "Or if the conversion to the metric system goes through in time, the Daytona 804.672."

LARRY DREW II BACK WITH UNC TAR HEELS
MARCH 24, 2011

One of the strangest events in UNC basketball history has just gotten stranger.

For those of you who don't know, Larry "Midnight Mover" Drew II, left the UNC Tar Heels in the middle of the season. Apparently, Drew and/or his parents got their lip pooched out when he lost his starting position, so instead of working to get his spot back, he wrapped his belongings (rumored to be nothing more than a half-eaten Snickers bar and a copy of Martina McBride's first album on cassette) in a handkerchief, tied it to the end of a stick and hopped on a turnip truck headed for Monterey.

Since Drew's departure, the worst thing to happen to the Tar Heels is their 1-2 record against Duke. Add to that an injury that has sidelined Kinston's own Reggie Bullock and the Tar Heels are now playing with a seven-man rotation, which makes their advance to this week's Sweet 16 all the more impressive.

While the Tar Heels have somehow managed to thrive with a depleted lineup, Larry Drew II hasn't faired as well. Since his disappearance, various rumors have surfaced in regards to his whereabouts.

One report said Drew had become a recruiter for the Church of Scientology due to Drew's thetan status as an Amway salesman during his previous life on Saturn. A source inside the Republican Party has been quoted as saying Drew may be gearing up to make a vice presidential run alongside Newt Gingrich. Others say Drew has been sitting around in his sweats and playing Xbox for the past month.

While details on Drew's activities during the month following his departure are murky at best, it seems Drew has been making overtures towards his former team as of late. First came Drew's rap version of the "Tar Heel Stomp" that surfaced on YouTube last week, followed shortly by an appearance on "The View" where Drew could be seen using sign language to spell out the phrase "PLEASE TAKE ME BACK ROY" while Joy Behar proceeded to eat a live beagle puppy and blame Sarah Palin for the stock market crash of 1929.

The most shocking revelation came from the Orange County, Calif., Police Department Wednesday afternoon. According to a press release, a man fitting Drew's description allegedly boarded the team bus dressed as UNC Tar Heel mascot Rameses.

"I've been wearing the ram outfit at ball games for years," said UNC alum Brian Sutton. "My brother Mark used to do it, but he kept forgetting to take it off after the games."

In a statement given to the OCPD, Sutton said Larry Drew II stole the costume from him while he was waiting to board a plane to the Sweet 16 in Newark.

"He distracted me with a Snickers bar," Sutton said. "He just grabbed the Rameses costume and took off; on top of everything else, he'd already eaten half of the Snickers bar."

Authorities in Newark say they plan to question whoever is wearing the UNC ram suit at the game on Friday. If the person wearing the costume is in fact Drew, authorities say he will be arrested unless coach Roy Williams believes his jump shot has markedly improved since February.

NEW WAITING PERIOD FOR ALL KITCHEN PURCHASES
APRIL 07, 2011

Within the space of a month, the Greene County Sheriff's Office has reported two assaults that involved kitchen utensils.

In Tuesday's edition of The Free Press, crime reporter Wesley Brown wrote about a mother and daughter who were arrested for allegedly attacking a neighbor with a fork and steak knife; on Feb. 22, he wrote about a Maury inmate allegedly attacking another with a plastic rolling pin.

With an angry public looking for answers, local authorities have decided to take drastic action.

"There are laws on the books that require citizens to wait a certain number of days to buy a gun," said Sgt. Kate Middleton of the Greene County Police Department. "We've decided to enact a three-day waiting period for all kitchen related purchases."

Middleton said since she joined the force in 2003, she has investigated hundreds of attacks involving steak knives, forks, pasta strainers, lettuce crispers — and in one case, a roll of aluminum foil.

"These things usually don't go to trial," Middleton said. "More often than not, a wife has grown weary of their husband's boorish behavior during supper, and since this usually happens in the kitchen, they are more likely to grab the nearest blunt object and fling it at their significant other's head.

"Usually, the men are too embarrassed to admit having their tater torn up by a 130-pound woman armed with a cheese grater."

While most men in the Greene County area are in favor of the new waiting period, on the whole, women see the new law as an unneeded nuisance.

"The other night, my husband Earl thought it'd be funny to 'kill a few frogs' while we were trying to eat supper," said Natalie Maines of Snow Hill. "Anybody that does that while everybody is trying to eat collards deserves to be hit in the head with a blender full of pennies."

The new law – which goes into effect April 15 – has caused a rush on all kitchen-related retail stores.

"We haven't been this busy since those new Leon Spinks grills came out back in '07," said Virginia Madsen of The Melted Spatula in Snow Hill. "A couple of college kids always show up during rush week to buy melon ballers because they totally misunderstand what they're used for, but this new law has been great for business. We even sold that molcajete that's been in the back since 1985."

Neil Innes of the N.T.A. (National Tong Association) says the law will only drive potential consumers to the black market.

"Say a woman has a dinner party coming up Friday night," Innes said. "It's the night before the party; she watches Martha Stewart and realizes her salad tongs aren't as shiny as Martha's. Her choices are to go to the store and be allowed to pick up her new tongs on Monday, or she can go down to that gas station out where the buses don't run and buy a pair of tongs from some shady character wearing a trench coat and a Duke T-shirt."

Innes says buying kitchen utensils from the black market is a risky proposition.

"We get reports of injuries resulting from shoddy equipment all the time," Innes said. "Just last week, a high school student who was making a cake for a home economics class had to be hospitalized after a whisk her parents bought her on the black market busted and became tangled in her braces.

"The poor thing was in the middle of a yawn, so it got hung up in there real good."

Middleton also provided a list of kitchen items that have been banned all together:
- Grape cubers
- Cheese peelers
- Air strainers
- Carrot waxers
- Cat fileters

Thanks to Free Press reporter Wes Brown for the head's up on the kitchen implement violence in Greene County.

CARS OVERTURNED AFTER KICKBALL VICTORY
APRIL 21, 2011

There are many items on the list of things in life that are worth getting worked up over — gas prices, taxes, the collection of bleeps and grunts on Bryan Hanks' iPod, and the fact Chris Brown has a career are near the top of mine.

There are many things worth getting your eggs boiled over, but I'll use what George Carlin referred to as "flawless logic" to let you in on a little secret: Kickball isn't one of them.

That's right, I said kickball. The Free Press has a kickball team that competes at the Fairfield Recreation Center on Tuesdays and Thursdays. I wasn't there when the charter for the team was written in lamb's blood on papyrus imported from Greece, but I believe the two main goals of forming the team were to get some exercise and have some fun.

In any competition, it's understandable that emotions may sometimes run high, especially if a championship or a large sum of money is on the line. When it comes to a pickup game of kickball, though, you'd think the participants would realize that it's KICKBALL and not the Super Bowl.

Case in point — during the inaugural game last week, Free Press photographer and president of the North Carolina Kenny Rogers Fan Club Janet Sutton Carter flew into an apoplectic rage when The Free Press lost to Mrs. Lolas Blizzard's kindergarten class. Most folks on the team simply enjoyed the camaraderie, but Janet huddled the team together and laid into them with a verbal tirade that was equal parts "Knute Rockne Story," Dick Vitale's "Tough People Survive Tough Times" speech, and Christian Bale hitting an assistant with a phone because his latte was too warm.

"I didn't come out here to lose," Janet told the startled Free Press squad as they tried to avert her steely gaze. "This was pure foolishness."

I opted not to play kickball, for I knew that somebody would get all berserk and think the outcome of the game actually mattered. Little did I know that person would be Janet Sutton Carter, a woman who didn't even stop drinking her Sprite while Judy Strickland from the advertising department recently beat Bryan Hanks within an inch of his life with a 1999 Greene County phone book.

"It didn't concern me," Janet told the investigating officer. "Those drinks are too expensive to waste and I'm not even Bryan's blood type."

This week, the ballin' express known as The Free Press took on Scott Alston and the Kinston Parks and Recreation team in what was dubbed "The War near the Store" at Fairfield. The loose, happy feel of the previous week had been replaced by darkness and tension that was no doubt brought on by Janet's intimidation tactics.

"She was calling us at all hours of the night," said reporter/second baseman David Anderson. "She'd blow a whistle and make us do push-ups over the phone."

By all accounts, The Free Press team was more focused this time out, but they still lost 16-4. While Janet had to be escorted to her car after trying to drown Richard Clark of the universal desk in a water fountain for falling down during the game, the rest of the team seemed pleased with their improved performance.

Unnamed members of the Parks and Recreation squad were so elated at their superior ball-kicking abilities that they overturned several cars, started a bonfire and broke into an a cappella version of Justin Bieber's "Eennie Meenie" while they roasted marshmallows over a smoldering Toyota.

The next morning, Janet waxed philosophical about the previous evening's events.

"Everybody gave me a hard time about my desire to win," Janet said. "I just thought they were all soft, that is until I saw a guy from the Parks and Recreation Department jump up on a fence and act like a lunatic because they won a kickball game ... a kickball game; pure foolishness."

Was there a lesson learned here? Probably not, although Janet has vowed to never again commit a misdemeanor in the name of kicking a rubber bag of air.

What about the guy who lost his mind and climbed the fence? Well that young man grew up to be country music-singing sensation Conway Twitty.

And now you have the rest of the story — good day.

BIN LADEN'S DUPLIN COUNTY RELATIVE SPEAKS OUT
MAY 05, 2011

While news of Osama Bin Laden's death has dominated the national spotlight, the passing of the terrorist mastermind hits close to home for one of his distant cousins living in Duplin County.

"I don't condone what he did, but he was still family," said Leroy Bin Laden, 48, of Albertson. "I hadn't seen him since a family reunion at White Lake in 1974."

Leroy says his cousin Osama left the reunion early due to a disagreement over the menu.

"I told him before he got here to expect a traditional southern pig pickin'," Leroy said. "He got one look at that barbecue and flew into a rage. I told him to just get some hush puppies and coleslaw but he wouldn't hear of it."

Communication with his famous cousin was rare after the barbecue incident.

"Every once in a while I'd get a birthday card from him," Leroy said. But even then he would sign it 'Happy Birthday to my favorite infidel; your homey, Osama.' He tried to be hip but it never really suited him."

The last time Leroy Bin Laden heard from his cousin was in 2008 when AFRO (American Flatulence Response Organization) agents believed Leroy was planning an airborne attack at a Larry The Cable Guy concert in Duplin County.

"Those charges were eventually dropped," Leroy said as he adjusted his Jihad 'er Done! T-shirt. "Yes, I did go around buying up collards, but as I told the authorities at the time, I only bought them because I was trying to make a poor man's sauna. I couldn't afford one of those fancy machines that makes the bubbles, so I had to improvise."

For his part, Leroy isn't quite so sure Osama is actually dead.

"We haven't seen a picture, a video — nothing that definitively proves they turned him into shark bait," Leroy said. "I've been getting emails from

154

somebody called 'notosama99@gmail.com' for the last few days. I'm not saying it's him – I'm just sayin' it could be."

Leroy said 'notosama99@gmail' told him he is in the country and looking for work.

"From what I can tell, he's somewhere in Texas right now," Leroy said. "He said something about coming to Kinston to get a job at Sanderson, but he's worried they won't let him wear his turban for safety reasons. He only wears it because he's got a bald spot up there the size of hubcap; you wouldn't think somebody who spent so much time in caves would be so vain."

When asked if he had anything in common with is cousin, Leroy Bin Laden said they both have a soft spot for a certain chanteuse.

"If he gets here in time, we're totally going to see Barbra Streisand in Vegas," Leroy said in a voice that was a few clicks higher than normal for an adult male. "He wouldn't admit to it, but Osama loves nothing more than curling up on the couch with a box of Kleenex and watching 'Yentil'; he also believes the relationship between Jackie Gleason and Burt Reynolds in 'Smokey and the Bandit' is a metaphor for the Middle East's struggle against the tyranny of the United States and their allies."

Leroy Bin Laden – currently employed as a customer greeter at "The John Edwards House of Homemade Erotica and Taxidermy" in Wilmington — is currently working on a screenplay about his life.

"It's called 'Jihad 'er Done, Jihad 'er Done, Pass the Biscuits and Load Your Guns,' and we're hoping to get either Aaron Sorkin or Oliver Stone involved in the project," Leroy said. "It's the type of movie that needs a self-important prong at the helm to capture the true bin Laden essence."

WNCT, WCTI AND WITN TO MERGE
(UPDATED WITH WCTI RESPONSE)
APRIL 01, 2011

Newspapers and adult-themed water parks are not the only businesses feeling the pinch of tough economic times; Late Thursday afternoon, it was announced that Eastern North Carolina's three television stations would merge.

According to a joint press release from the three stations, WNCT CBS-9, WCTI ABC-12 and WITN NBC-7 will merge into one station — to be called WICN 28 —April 15. The release states the merger was brought about by "tough economic times" and one executive's "compulsive need to see WCTI's Valentina Wilson in that red dress as often as possible."

Still to be determined is who will be the anchorman for the 6 o'clock news.

"Allan Hoffman has seniority, but Wes Goforth and Dave Jordan have large followings as well," said Graham Chapman of "What's On" magazine. "I've heard rumblings the new WICN will start with a three-man news team and viewers will be able to text their vote for favorite. Whoever gets the most votes will anchor the 6 o'clock report, while the other two anchors will cover the evening news reports at 4, 4:15, 5, 5:30, 5:45 and 5:55."

According to Michael Palin of "Weatherperson Weekly," the weatherman/woman will be chosen based on the condition of their respective Dopplers.

"In the TV weather game it all comes down to who has the best Doppler," Chapman said. "Skip Waters and David Sawyer talk a good game, but word around the water cooler is that Marvin Daugherty's Doppler is the one to beat."

Each station has its own meteorological vocabulary, but the new WICN plans to streamline the terminology.

"Back in the old days when Jim Woods was doing the weather with a dry erase board and a magic marker, we used archaic terms such as 'rain,' 'snow' and 'windy,' " said Terry Gilliam of WNCT. "Once everybody started flaunting their Dopplers, we updated our vocabulary to meet the needs of today's overeducated viewer."

Gilliam provided the following chart to illustrate the evolution of weather terminology:

1930–1985	1985–2010	2011
Snow	Winter weather event	Solstice hootenanny
Rain	Rain event	Angel tears
Windy	Windy conditions	Negative stillness ratio
Tornado	Funnel cloud	Cantankerous wind mass

While official numbers are unavailable, experts predict this consolidation will leave upwards of 46 people without a job — 12 of whom were in charge of scouring newspaper websites for stories.

"There is no need to panic," said John Jones of the Measley Media Group. "People reading this should realize it's April 1."

You can't reach Staff Writer Dawn Johnson at The Free Press, because frankly, she doesn't exist. Happy April Fool's Day.

CSS NEUSE II STOLEN
CIVIL WAR REPLICA LAST SEEN HEADED TO
THE COAST ON U.S. 70
APRIL 01, 2009

One of Kinston's biggest tourist attractions was stolen Tuesday afternoon.

According to an incident report obtained from the Lenoir County Sheriff's Office, the CSS Neuse II gunboat - a replica of the CSS Neuse that is housed on Vernon Avenue - was taken from the corner of Herritage and Gordon.

"We're looking at security tapes from local businesses," Lenoir County Sheriff Billy Smith said.

Eyewitnesses reported a large white truck backed up to the boat and started attaching harnesses to the hull around 2 p.m.

"The guy driving the truck said they were taking the boat down to the river for the Festival on The Neuse," Jeremy Simpson said.

Simpson, who saw the activity around the boat as he was on his way back from a lunch break, said the group of workers seemed to be reporting to a woman in her mid to late 50s.

"There was a very official-looking woman who was giving orders and carrying a clipboard," Simpson said. "She seemed to be a bit agitated, but nothing seemed out of the ordinary."

Witnesses reported that on the way out of town, the thieves went through a Kinston restaurant's drive-through, causing significant damage.

"We were sitting at Right Way eating dinner, and all of a sudden we saw this huge truck pull into the drive way with a large boat behind it," said Morty Bluth, a retired school teacher from Boston. "We came down here for a few weeks vacation on the Outer Banks; we just assumed it was an ark that was built for a parade."

Damage estimates to the drive-through roof were not available at press time.

Charles Lawson of Deep Run said he and his family witnessed the boat as it headed down U.S. 70.

"We thought it was odd that a large gunboat would have a 'My Grandson is a Super Student at La Grange Elementary' sticker on the back," Lawson said.

Calls swamped the Sheriff's Office all afternoon. Citizens also sent pictures from their cell phones and digital cameras to law enforcement agencies.

"A picture was taken at the stoplight near the tobacco warehouses on U.S. 70 West," Smith said. "They also said the large truck seemed to be following a small, white Toyota pick-up truck with blue lettering on the side."

The replica of the Ram Neuse was constructed by master boat builder Alton Stapleford of Kinston.

"I guess I forgot to lock it," Stapleford said. "My bad."

If you have any information about the theft of the CSS Neuse, please realize that it's April Fools Day.

Dave Allan Goforth can be reached at (252) 559-1040.

14 WOMEN CLAIM AFFAIRS WITH SANTA
DECEMBER 17, 2009

What was once an unfounded rumor is now being treated as fact.

For years, there have been whispers of Santa Claus having affairs with various women all over the world.

"We noticed that it was taking him longer and longer to make the toy run every year," said Blitzen, a long-time collaborator. "Rudolph gave the old man a bottle of Viagra as a joke one year, and I guess he got curious."

According to the North Pole Gazette, on Nov. 23, Santa got into his 2009 Ford Escasleigh and sped out of his driveway while Mrs. Claus chased after him with a giant candy cane. After traveling only approximately 100 feet from his home, Santa struck a fire hydrant.

A neighbor told the Gazette that the vehicle's windows were smashed out, even though the impact of the vehicle against the hydrant was minor.

"Santa crawled out of his truck and laid in the snow," said an elf who asked not to be identified. "I went up to help him and I could definitely smell eggnog on his breath."

In an official statement posted on his Web site, Santa wrote:

"There's no question about it, Santa has been very naughty this year. For years when I exclaimed 'ho-ho-ho,' everybody thought it was an exclamation, but it was actually a request. The sad fact of the matter is that milk and cookies just don't get it done any more, and the ability to disappear up a chimney in a matter of seconds just made my transgressions even more exciting. I've decided to take a hiatus from delivering toys this year, so the Easter Bunny, Batman and Kanye West have agreed to help get the toys out to all the girls and boys."

In the days since this stunning revelation, several women have claimed to have been a paramour of Mr. Claus.

"Yeah, we had some fun together," The Tooth Fairy said. "Those elves of his used to get drunk and fight all the time; if teeth got knocked out he'd pick 'em up and put them under his pillow just so I'd show up."

Along with The Tooth Fairy, female managers of 13 different Toys 'R Us stores have come forward to say they had daliances with the red-suited jelly belly.

"A few years ago when the elves were threatening to go union, he came in the store to set up an account," said Stephanie Reynolds, 34, of Toys 'R Us in Seattle. "He kept pointing to his mistletoe belt buckle; he was quite the charmer."

While several famous women and Rosie O'Donnell have lambasted Santa in the press, Tiger Woods and David Letterman have publicly thrown their support behind the philandering fat man. Several of Santa's sponsors have dropped him from their campaigns, but industry sources say Santa is a shoo-in to become the spokesman for Alltel's new "No Tell" cell phone.

"The Alltel 'No Tell' phone features the new Hide-a-Skank™ technology," company spokesman Frank Gifford said. "If your mistress calls you on the 'No Tell' phone, the screen will display the number of the local dry cleaners, and her voice will be altered to sound like James Earl Jones."

The Alltel 'No Tell' is expected to hit the market in January.

FALSE RAPTURE CAUSES LOCAL MAN TO MAIM HIMSELF
MAY 24, 2011

Radio personality Harold Camping's prediction that the world would end on May 21 didn't come true, but things have definitely taken a downward turn for one Lenoir County resident.

"I really thought this was the big one," said Alfred Sanford of Little Baltimore. "I've still got a few cases of Spam left over from the Rapture of '94. I guess I'll be sprinklin' Spam on my Tony flakes for a little while longer."

Sanford was so sure the end was coming he decided to quit his job of 28 years — just one year shy of retirement. The day Sanford announced he was leaving is not one his former co-workers will soon forget.

"I don't know how he did it, but he somehow covered his entire buttockle area with lip gloss," said Sanford's former supervisor Eddie Long of Allco Electric. "When the lights struck it the right way, it would almost blind you; it looked like Andy Rooney eating a lemon."

According to Long, Sanford went around the office telling everybody where they could go and what they could cram where when they got there. Although one double-jointed warehouse worker without a working knowledge of sarcasm carried out many of Sanford's wishes, the rest reportedly just looked on in disbelief.

"It was not lip gloss," Sanford said. "I thought it was lip balm; as it turns out they now make Crazy Glue in tubes that look a lot like Chap Stick. Before I could get to a shower, lots of nooks and crannies got sealed up, and I'm presently in day four of what the guy in the emergency room called a 'dyspeptic episode'."

Doctors warned Sanford that in his current state, one bite of a burrito could result in his knee caps being blown off.

With the world coming to an end in a day and his backside now transmogrified into a large, fleshy Weeble Wobble version of a 2-year-old that won't open up for a spoonful of carrots, Sanford decided to max out his credit card.

"I've always loved Krispy Kreme doughnuts," Sanford said, as he eased himself down into a wash tub full of paint thinner. "Since the world was coming to an end, I went over to Goldsboro and bought everything they had — doughnuts, coffee, napkins — they even threw in the pimply-faced skateboard punks who were loitering in the parking lot."

When asked how many he was able to eat, Sanford simply shook his head.

"I only ate three," Sanford said. "I emptied the rest of them in the tub and just rolled around in 'em for a few hours. It's a shame what happened to them éclairs."

Sanford was subsequently charged with misdemeanor crimes against pastry by the La Grange Police Department.

LEFTY'S RESTAURANT EXPECTS
WARMED-OVER WELCOME IN KINSTON
MAY 26, 2011

If you're a restaurateur in Kinston, you're probably sleeping with one eye open these days. The Broken Eagle is the latest to succumb, and the rumor mill is rife with news that other closings are on the way.

While most sane people would shy away from opening a new restaurant during one of the worst economies since Jimmy Carter's brother relieved himself in front of a slew of reporters, Hines Ward believes he has a concept that is recession proof.

"When I was growing up we always ate leftovers," Ward said. "If we had shepherd's pie on Monday you could bet your sweet bippy you'd see it again on Tuesday. Since most Americans eat leftovers, I thought it would be a good idea to open a leftover-themed restaurant."

The restaurant — which will be called "Lefty's" — will be Hines' second attempt at culinary success.

"I opened a Lefty's in Washington, D.C., back in 2003," Ward said. "Republicans refused to eat there because of the name, and the Democrats boycotted us because they thought we were discriminating against right-handed people."

To dispel any misconceptions about Lefty's, Ward is buying newspaper ads and radio time to let people know what his restaurant is all about.

"Say you have hamburgers on Wednesday night, and there are three left over," Ward said. "If you don't want to eat hamburgers again that week, all you have to do is use our drive-thru window on your way to work. Someone from our staff will weigh your leftovers and pay you $1.50 per pound."

Lefty's, on Vernon Avenue between Hardee's and McDonald's, opened on May 24 to rave reviews.

"The service is really fast because the food has already been cooked," said Lefty's customer Haney Ginsburg of Grifton. "I got some hamburger steak that had a few cigarette ashes on top, just like mama used to make."

While Lefty's looks like it could weather the bad economy, Ward admits that some people have tried to take advantage of his new business model.

"We caught a couple of truants going through the soup kitchen line and bringing the food over here to sell," Ward said. "I know the police are busy, so I made them go out and bring back a switch. You just can't beat the compassionate discipline of a well-formed magnolia limb."

Being this is the South, the biggest sellers at Lefty's so far have been collards, squash and fried chicken.

"I had to pull out my pistol the other day when a guy from PETA came in here with some tofu," Ward said. "That mess looked like the salve we used to put on the diseased part of a mule's butt."

If Lefty's is a success Hines plans to open a retread-only tire shop, a used but not abused underwear boutique and a dating service for women who've recently lowered their standards.

"There are plenty of single and/or divorced men in Lenoir County that need women to take care of them," Ward said. "If you're a single woman looking for an average fella to keep the grass cut and keep his trap shut during 'Dancing with the Stars,' I've got several men for you to choose from. Most of them are a little paunchy and have lost some hair, but the majority of them have passed their emissions tests. Several have less than 100,000 miles on them, although a few do have problematic transmissions."

COMMENCEMENT ADDRESS GIVEN
BY HOURLY EMPLOYEE
JUNE 14, 2011

Congratulations on graduating high school. That cap and gown that was worn once and cost $60 will be crammed in a box that will eventually be tossed in the landfill when you clean out your attic in 2031. But I'm sure you looked great in it for that one hour.

When I graduated from North Lenoir High School, a few buddies and I realized the cap and gown deal was a scam, so we chipped in and bought one. As one of us left the stage after receiving our diploma, we immediately took off the cap and gown and passed it down to the next guy. After graduation, we cut it down the middle and used it as a tent at the beach that weekend. Later that night, our friend Mike Gagliano came down with a case of Schnoinkel fever, so we wrapped him in the tattered graduation gown, lit a few candles and played Sarah McLachlan albums until he came to.

The main problem with these commencement speeches is that they always get somebody incredibly successful to deliver them. Many people have come from virtually nothing and worked their way to the top of their profession by climbing the ladder one difficult step after another. On the other hand, there are also a good number of people who rode the escalator of cronyism and nepotism to the top without breaking a sweat.

Thankfully, East Lenoir High School decided to balance things out a little bit this year by hiring Keith Emerson — a $9.75/hour building maintenance man — to deliver the commencement address. The following is a portion of that address:

"I want to thank the East Lenoir administration for asking me to speak to you today. Usually around this time, I'd be scrubbing the toilets down after everybody in the office got back from a 12-bean burrito lunch, so this is a nice change of scenery and a moderate improvement in odor.

"Twenty years ago I was just like you — young, ambitious and full of hope. I attended a local state university for four years, and while my grades didn't exactly cause Stephen Hawking to fall out of his chair, I was a solid B-student. After completing my college education, I came back to Lenoir County armed with a college diploma, a resume that made Warren Buffet look like a parking attendant and a spiffy $100 suit from the Wearhouse for Men.

"For the next few months, I went on what felt like hundreds of job interviews. In some cases I didn't get the job because I wasn't willing to relocate three times within the next decade. Finally, it looked like a car rental firm was going to put me in charge of their local branch. I was told to be ready to go to Raleigh in a few weeks for training, which to me made it sound like a done deal.

"But fate intervened in the form of a higher-up in the company — a higher up who just happened to be a former member of a popular fraternity at a local university known for drinking and tearing up football stadiums after victories. According to the woman who had already promised me the job, she received a phone call from the higher-up urging her instead to hire the son of a fellow frat-brother that needed work. Apparently, he'd been arrested for driving while impaired a few times and he was having a hard time finding a job. I myself made it through college without ingesting anything stronger than a Pepsi, but that didn't seem to matter.

"A few years later, I saw her and asked how things were going. She said she spent most of her time cleaning up messes made by Son of Frat Boy. To add insult to injury, the frat boy in question was now making more than she was, even though she was technically his boss. She's complained as much as she can without getting fired, and with the economy in the septic tank she has no choice but to put up with it.

"Although it's been many years since the drunk party boy yanked the job out from under me, it still angers me to this day. In fact, if I'm walking through a parking lot and happen to see a car from this rental company, I make it a point to kick the passenger door at least six times. It doesn't make up for what happened, but it sure makes me feel better and it helps keep those knee joints loosey-goosey.

"In closing, remember that if you work hard and keep your nose clean there is still a decent chance that you'll get shafted. My advice to you is to convince a member of a far-reaching fraternity or politically powerful family to adopt you. This may not be the ethical or moral thing to do, but by the time you enter the job market, gas will be $6/gallon, and business is business."

To book Mr. Emerson to speak at your event, contact his agent at the number listed below.

GRANDMA GETS DOWN BUT CAN'T GET UP
JULY 05, 2011

Although it's totally against my nature, I actually went out and mingled with other humans last Saturday night.

It all started when a musician buddy asked me to go with him to check out a band that was playing in Greenville. The band is called Green Turtle and they turned out to be quite good, but that's not the crux of this biscuit.

The band was playing at a hotel bar, and being a teetotaler, I have no interest in being surrounded by drunks. Beyond that, I despise having to yell to carry on a conversation.

I figured I'd be there trying to enjoy the music, only to constantly be interrupted by a recently divorced man in his early 50s who really wants to tell me how much he's enjoying the single life. This is the same guy who'll be crying like John Boehner Baker during a screening of "Sophie's Choice" after he's had about two beers.

As the band launched into "Bring On The Night" by The Police, a group of folks who were attending a family reunion at the hotel walked, sashayed and staggered into the bar. They were all wearing T-shirts that read "Campbell Family Reunion - Mmm Mmm Good," and they were ready for a good time. An older, distinguished member of the group ordered a Diet Coke and sat next to me and we chatted about how good the bass player was.

While my new friend was content to sit in a corner and enjoy the music, the rest of the Campbell family put on a crash course on life and how to live it with vivacity. As soon as the band launched into a trio of Bob Marley tunes, one of the more mature Campbell women made her way to the dance floor and proceeded to shake it, drop it, bend it, shuck it and twirl it. If she had it, it was in motion.

Seeing one of their own dance with such abandon apparently inspired the rest of the clan to strut their proverbial stuff with suitable aplomb. I'm not sure the good Lord intended for our vertebrae to bend into the shape of a question mark, but the Campbell Grandma at the center of the melee seemed to be channeling a bendy-straw in a blender.

At the end of her dance, Grandma Campbell got herself a rum and Coke and had a seat. Her family — although still laughing from her display — seemed relieved that she was seated and taking in much-needed fluids. No sooner had things calmed down when the band launched into "Brown Eyed Girl" and Grandma Campbell — drink in hand — headed back to the dance floor.

Apparently this alcohol stuff affects your motor skills, because the more Grandma Campbell sipped on what she referred to as her "drank," she started to bob and weave a little bit. I'm not referring to the bob and weave of Muhammad Ali or Joe Frazier, but more like that of Foster Brooks or Dudley Moore. Somehow, this innovative woman was able to walk at a 45 degree angle without spilling a drop of her drank.

After about three dranks, Grandma Campbell started the old "Drop it like it's hot" routine. She'd drop her formidable rear-end on the floor and prop herself up with her right hand whenever she did so. I'm sure that when she did this at the height of the disco era in 1977 it was a sight to see, but in the cold, harsh light of 2011, it looked like something Amnesty International would start a letter-writing campaign over. It was even rumored that FEMA was sending a team from Washington to shut the whole thing down.

Right in the middle of James Brown's "Get Up Offa That Thing," Grandma Campbell tempted fate one too many times and got hung up in the propped-buttocks position. As she sat there propped on one hand, (trying in vain to pretend she was staying down there for a long time for dramatic effect), the band mercilessly kept chanting the chorus: "Get up offa that thing/and dance till you feel better."

She kept yelling to the band that she couldn't get up, but they thought she was asking them to sing it again - which they did for another 10 minutes.

Though she made a valiant effort — and at one point was able to lift one cheek off the floor for a few seconds — it was not to be.

Younger members of the Campbell family were summoned to help get their inebriated elder off the floor. A couple of active duty Marines tried to lift Grandma off the floor to no avail. Eventually, somebody brought down a bed sheet, slid her on to it, and dragged Grandma Campbell through the hotel lobby towards the elevator, which at this time let out an audible gasp.

As various family members set up a complex system of ropes, pulleys, chains and jumper cables in an attempt to place Grandma Campbell inside the elevator, in a fit of self-preservation, the elevator kept trying to close its doors in protest.

Eventually, Grandma Campbell made it in and — after a 47-minute ride — was deposited on the second floor. The elevator suffered a hernia and is currently out of work on sick leave.

LOCAL GRANDMA CAMPING OUT FOR HARRY POTTER
JULY 14, 2011

Towns across the country will be crawling with Hufflepuffs and Voldemorts this weekend as the final "Harry Potter" movie swoops in to save Hollywood from being converted into a giant Jamba Juice.

Before asking a coworker about this phenomenon, I couldn't have told you the difference between a Harry Potter and a Balding Sculptor. To me, "Harry Potter" sounds like a dirty hippie that sells necklaces and weed out of a van at the beach.

Apparently, this Potter kid is some sort of wizard; the only wizard I know anything about plays a mean pinball from Soho down to Brighton. Even on my favorite table, he can beat my best – his disciples lead him in, and he just does the rest — but I digress.

The coworker I gleaned my Harry knowledge from is none other than local folk legend Paulette Burroughs. Burroughs — who just spent three months on the road as Kid Rock's personal tick checker — says she was introduced to the world of Harry Potter through her grandsons.

"My grandsons Kevin and Josh introduced me to the books," Paulette said. "I used to love Harry Potter when he was the colonel on 'M*A*S*H,' so I guess these stories about him as a young man are sort of a prequel."

Paulette became so enthralled with the story of the young wizard who fights Death Eaters during the Korean War that she's decided to camp outside the theater tonight to ensure she gets a ticket.

"I keep waiting for them to show him at the 4077th with Hawkeye and Hot Lips Houlihan," Burroughs said. "I guess they're saving that for the finale."

Hollywood insiders are predicting this installment of the Potter series could make it the most lucrative film of all-time, surpassing Star Wars and Corky Ramano.

"Along with ticket sales, you've got to consider all of the merchandising that is going on," said Irving Schnoinkel of Schnoinkel & Killete Artist

Representation and Taxidermy. "There's Harry Potter shirts, mugs, suppositories – talk about exploring a dark underworld."

Stephen Root of Pricehike Theatres says moviegoers will have the chance to enjoy some special Harry Potter-themed treats at the concession stand.

"We're selling a grey cotton candy called 'Dumbledore's Beard on a Stick'," Root said. "We've got Bertie Bott's flop-sweat flavored hot dogs; my personal favorite are the 'Hagrid's Toe-Jam Goobers', both with and without corn."

"I'll be setting up my tent at the theatre after work on Thursday," Burroughs said while packing her backpack full of supplies. "I've got everything I need in this bag to survive outside: freeze-dried water, a set of nun chucks, and a case of Luther Vandross CDs."

Burroughs says she's seen some crazy things while camping out for movie tickets.

"One time I was camped out next to this group of skeezy-looking folks," Burroughs said. "Not only did they have food and water in their tent, I saw a can of something called 'Panty Raid.' The slogan under the logo read: "If your draws are infested, our spray will digest it.'

"I tried some of it on a Ritz cracker, and it was pretty good."

Special thanks to Shana Norris for the crash course in Harry Potter. Original lyrics to "Pinball Wizard" by Pete Townshend.

DOLLY PARTON'S TRAINING BRA
FOUND IN LOCAL FLEA MARKET
JULY 19, 2011

This past Saturday morning, I gathered up tax deductions No. 1 and No. 2 and decided to take them to the closest thing we have to a museum in Lenoir County — the flea market.

Why do I attach such lofty praise upon what is essentially a group yard sale? Because flea markets are a sociological buffet for the common man, and since we of the hoi polloi are most certainly headed for lives that involve living in cars and skimming ditch banks for drinking water, we should start looking for bargains now.

Our flea market in La Grange has to be one of the most diverse in the country. Before we even made our way inside, we encountered vendors of various backgrounds who possessed disparate ideas about personal hygiene, selling everything from George Jones 8-track tapes to an egg carton full of used golf balls.

One woman was selling what she claimed was Dolly Parton's training bra. As proof, she provided a picture of herself standing at the front gate of Dollywood in Tennessee. She was only asking $7 for it, but I wanted to look around and make sure there wasn't a better celebrity-bra deal available before I committed.

Elsewhere in the parking lot, a man by the name of Coy (yes, he's one of the guys who replaced Bo and Luke on "The Dukes of Hazard" for a few hellish weeks back in 1982) was selling various collections of commemorative plates. Coy was scratching a bit as we approached his table that had a "We Put the Flea in Flea Market" banner hanging across the front. As expected, he had plenty of Lady Diana and Mr. T merchandise, but it was some of his more esoteric inventory that aroused my interest.

For example, I had no idea M.C. Hammer sanctioned a set of Royal Doulton figurines in the late 1980s/early 1990s. The set of four represents all stages of the apparently legit-enough-to-quit star's career: The first piece shows Hammer working at a hardware store during the day while perfecting his rhymes on lunch breaks; the second depicts him as a worldwide superstar with millions of dollars and just as many hangers-on; the third figurine is a striking re-enactment of Hammer's ill-fated attempt to sell himself as a hardcore rapper on Arsenio Hall's talk show; the fourth shows Hammer and Vanilla Ice egging Eminem's house while on their paper routes.

After a while, we ventured inside to escape the hot mid-morning sun. In the distance, we noticed a giant, propeller-sized warehouse fan blowing at full speed. Tax deduction No. 2 loves it when wind blows through her hair, so we walked over to the fan and, within seconds, her soft blond hair was reaching for the stars.

As we stood there, I noticed a rather robust aroma in the premises. It didn't necessarily smell bad, but there was nothing about it that made you want to bottle it either. The smell was stiff yet flamboyant — sort of politician/pimp hybrid, with a hint of ginger.

After walking past a few booths of used clothing and shoes, I realized what I was smelling: the funk of thousands of past souls, once safely contained in cardboard boxes in attics, now unleashed like whatever that thing was at the end of the first Indiana Jones movie.

Between the box of used protective cups from a Turkish prison's football team and a collection of work pants from a Canadian bacon factory in Houston, there were more herbs and spices flying around in there than the time Colonel Sanders got drunk and crawled into the dryer.

I did run up on a booth that had some cool vinyl records for sale, and a nice man gave the tax deductions a free stuffed animal each.

As we made our way to the back of the store, I noticed the greatest display in the history of all retail. What I'm about to describe has not been embellished in any way. I didn't get the name of the vendor, but I'm sure someday his name will be on a plaque outside a government building or highway rest area.

The following is a list of the contents of the table as they were displayed in a left to right fashion: strawberries, bananas, kiwi, grapes, cantaloupes, polka-dot bras with pictures of fruit on them.

I don't know if this guy is Sigmund Freud's nephew or just a good ol' boy who likes his melons and his bras, but I ended up buying one of each — on principle.

After leaving the flea market, I drove the tax deductions to the Dollar Store, which they believe is actually a Toys-R-Us. I'm not sure why they think the Dollar Store is a Toys-R-Us, but it may have something to do with the fact that I've always told them that the Dollar Store was actually a Toys-R-Us.

The oldest tax deduction is doing quite well with her reading and is starting to ask questions, but it was a good ride while it lasted.

I was only in the store to get a few essentials: batteries, dog biscuits and — since I have an anniversary coming up — a can of silly string. A few rows over, I could hear an adult telling a group of kids to buy some snacks before they went around to the corner cinema to take in a movie.

I can't blame anyone for this, as the last time I went to a movie I had to sell two tires off of my car to pay for popcorn and a beverage.

Apparently, each kid was given $5, and the one closest to me picked up a bag of candy, a soda, a hardback copy of Michael Vick's Guide to Dog Care (to read during the 45-minutes worth of movie previews), an inflatable ashtray and an okra cozy with a Smurf on it.

With taxes on the rise and pay on the decline, it's only a matter of time before we turn into a nation of car-sleepers and ditch-crashers, but don't let that get you down. For the few pennies you'll be able to beg for or steal from underneath the drive-thru window of your nearest fast food restaurant, you can have all the junk food, bad literature and supportive undergarments you'll ever need.

GOD CERTAINLY IS FUNNY, AIN'T HE?
AUGUST 04, 2011

For those of you wishing for a story about Paulette punching a Shriner, you're out of luck this week. Life is too short to dwell on the foibles of the unstable among us, even if they do stuff that makes us laugh till Shasta squirts out of our nose.

No, I've decided to start using this space for bigger issues — and as issues go, they don't get any bigger than God.

The focus of this week's scripture is God's sense of humor. Before any of the zealots in the congregation start placing an order for a quart of lamb's blood to throw at me, just hear me out. To quote Proverbs 17:22: "A joyful heart is good medicine, but a crushed spirit dries up the bones."

For one thing, since an early age, I've been taught we were created in God's image. By that logic, if we enjoy a good laugh, then surely the Big Guy must enjoy a good knee-slapper every once in a while himself.

Just look at most sermons — the preacher usually starts things out with a joke. When I was about 14 a preacher named Joe Donakey told the following joke during a sermon: "What was the first car mentioned in the Bible? A Honda — because the Apostles were all in one Accord."

That stinker — which I thoroughly enjoyed — elicited the loudest collective groan I've ever heard in a church. The second loudest came when someone suggested doing away with covered dish dinners. The person who suggested that was subsequently banned from the property; we Methodists are a kind bunch, but we do have our limits.

Can I get an amen?

In my personal life, I see God's humor every day in the form of a blond, diapered midget/monkey that runs around my house like a chimp on banana day at the zoo. She's about 16 months old and has enough energy to power a nuclear submarine. She laughs easy, loves to dance and — based on her love of getting into everything and climbing — she'll either be an architect or a roofer.

Sure, that sounds like a normal baby, but her soon-to-be 7-year-old sister was quite different at that age. She had boundless energy, but developed a good sense of boundaries early on. Every night around 7:30, she'd crawl up into a ball like a cat and go to sleep.

This newer model has to be coerced, tricked and caressed into sleeping. When our first daughter went to sleep, you could vacuum in the room she was sleeping in and she wouldn't wake up. The new one will wake up if one of us simply thinks about making a noise.

Why is this funny? Because God sandbagged us, that's why. Before we had tax deduction No. 1, we were told the following ad nauseum: "Your life is over," "You'll never sleep again," "Start drinking now."

But raising tax deduction No. 1 wasn't that bad. Aside from the occasional bad cold or scraped knee, it was a piece of cake compared to what we were expecting.

After having such a relatively easy time with tax deduction No. 1, we decided to bring tax deduction No. 2 into the picture. Well, she's here now and she's great, but my wife and I believe she's slowly and methodically trying to kill us both.

I think she wants the house, and we've shown her the mortgage to let her know that if she bumps us off, she'll have 27 years of payments on her shoulders. She glanced over it but then went back to taking the washing machine apart.

God saw that we thought we had it all figured out, so to amuse himself he sent us a cute, drooling tree-swinger with advanced motor skills and a knack for demolition beyond her years. Good one, Big Guy.

IRENE BROUGHT OUT THE GOOD,
THE BAD AND THE UGLY
SEPTEMBER 01, 2011

Tragedies supposedly bring out the best in people, but I'm not so sure.

As Hurricane Irene retraced Sherman's ascent to the north, people huddled around radios as if it were the 1940s and FDR was giving a fireside chat. Local weathermen whipped out their Dopplers and Vipers for all to see, and from what I could see, people really seemed mesmerized.

Speaking of local TV news, is it me or are these stations just crawling with babes? When I was growing up, all we had was Slim Short and Jim Woods; now it's hard to focus on the news because the wimmens reading the news are so gosh-darn purdy. For a while Saturday, I plum forgot there was a hurricane going on.

You local TV station managers have quite a racket going on.

Aside from regenerating interest in terrestrial radio and climate moderation, not much good came from Irene. I'm sure there are isolated stories of kindness and bravery floating around out there, but the majority of emotion created from power outages and carnage is usually negative.

On Saturday after the power went out, local radio stations began carrying the audio feeds of local TV broadcasts. Every so often, the radio stations would break away and take calls from listeners with a story to tell. During one such segment, the radio host asked listeners to call in with their storm stories, and — without fail — seven people called in and said the same thing: "We've had a lot of rain and it's real windy."

Caller after caller took the time to use up the few remaining telephone lines that were still standing to state what the Webster's Dictionary of Duh describes as "The Obvious." After 20 minutes of "it's real windy" calls, the radio host alerted listeners that we all knew it was windy, and to only call if something unique had happened.

Heeding this instruction, the next caller told the radio host the wind was so bad at his house that it blew a rooster into a Coke bottle.

At my house, it got a little boring. The power was out and the humidity index was somewhere between a sauna and a tent preacher's armpit. Our oldest tax deduction decided to occupy her time by finding out how many licks it actually took to get to the center of a Tootsie Pop. Do you know how many licks it takes? Boy I sure do.

Like most of you, we had some trees come down during the storm, which just goes to show how pompous and petty they can be. A massive tree that could potentially cut through the middle of a brick house as if it were warm butter can't stand up to a little wind — what piffle. The next time Arbor Day rolls around, I suggest FEMA pass out chainsaws to anyone and everyone who's willing to do a little pre-hurricane tree thinning.

As most adults with at least a third-grade education should have done, I put gas in my car before the storm hit. That being said, on Monday, I noticed most of the stations were out of gas, so when I finally saw one that was open, I decided to get a little more. As I attempted to pull into the gas station, I noticed two brain surgeons were blocking the entrance to the station. They just sat there in their trucks with the windows down having a conversation about something vital to national security, I'm sure.

I pulled up behind these two Mensa charter members thinking that would be the cue for them to skedaddle, but to no avail. I then tooted the horn, which also fell on deaf ears. Finally, one of them turned and looked at me and asked me what I needed. I replied that it would be quicker for me to drive up to the pump instead of parking my car on the highway and then having to build an elaborate aqueduct system on the spot that would transport the gas from the pump, over his car and into mine.

Carl Sagan, Jr. took a second to mull over what I said and then got mad because he thought I accused him of looking like a duck. I then made a few derogatory remarks about his ancestry, and even questioned whether or not some of his kin may have stepped outside of their species for untoward recreational activities.

Confused, he thanked me for my apology and let me in.

One act of kindness that did occur was when Free Press Associate Managing Editor Nancy Saunders allowed Managing Editor Bryan Hanks and his horde of reporters to work out of her house while The Free Press office was without power. Sure, it resulted in some minor property damage and a few restraining orders, but — in theory — it went well.

LOCAL GAY MAN SPEAKS OUT AGAINST GAY MARRIAGE
SEPTEMBER 20, 2011

Simon Billings, 43, of Kinston, is on his way to becoming a partner at Ironside, Mason and Matlock. He enjoys football and has been known to bust out an impressive rendition of "Foggy Mountain Breakdown" on the banjo. His favorite restaurant is the Golden Corral buffet, and on more than one occasion has ended a bar fight by stacking his opponents in a cordwood-like fashion in the parking lot.

"Life's been going pretty good for me as of late," Billings said. "That was until this whole gay marriage thing came up."

Billings — who is gay — is adamantly against the legalization of gay marriage.

"I believe marriage should be between a man and a woman," Billings said. "I have no interest in spending my Saturdays at the Pottery Barn or doing any of that couple-stuff straight people are sentenced to; I'm gay, but I'm not GAY."

Billings has been in a committed relationship with Jones County roofer Arnold Layne since 2008.

"Arnold and I get along pretty good most of the time," Billings said. "He thinks I have far too much Loretta Lynn on my iPod, but other than that, it's pretty much smooth sailing."

While the majority of the gay community has been fighting to gain the right to marry, Billings said he's never believed it was a good idea.

"As a lawyer, I've seen many relationships end in divorce, and in most cases, at least one person ends up losing half their stuff," Billings said. "Arnold has been on me about getting married for a while, but since North Carolina doesn't recognize gay marriage, I've always felt like there was enough of a buffer to keep me from having to make things legal."

He continued: "I love Arnold like a play cousin, but I don't think a judge should be able to award him my entire Ric Flair commemorative plate collection just because we're not in love anymore; Arnold sure didn't spend all those Saturdays sifting through yard sales and flea markets to complete the set."

Layne said he and Billings started dating after a chance meeting at a Nickelback concert.

"Our seats were next to each other at the concert," Layne recalled. "I remarked how awful the band was and yelled out, 'They should rename this band I Want My Nickel And The Other $39.95 Back'. He told me how he loved a catty man in a Metallica T-shirt; before long, we were an item."

Layne said his coworkers seem to have accepted his sexuality.

"I work with a bunch of open-minded guys," Layne said of his fellow roofers. "Also, I'm the guy with the nail gun, so if they start giving me any crap I fire a warning shot over their head; that usually brings the overall tolerance level of the group up to an acceptable level."

"On a Sunday afternoon, all I want to do is lay on the couch with a beer and take in some figure skating like any normal guy," Billings said. "Arnold always wants to get dressed up and go mingle with the straights at Walmart, which on my bucket list is somewhere between gnawing on barbed wire and trying to figure out if Anderson Cooper and Rachel Maddow are the same person. Some straight people are cool I guess, but seeing a man and woman together that way is just weird."

Dexter Thompson is a professional marriage counselor and amateur taxidermist in Beulaville.

"The dynamics of a gay couple versus those of a straight couple are quite different," Thompson said as he stuffed a deer, bear and beaver for a local hunting club. "In a straight relationship, it's usually the woman who is trying to pin down the man; with a gay couple, you've got one guy trying to pin down another guy.

"While that may be an unfortunate turn of phrase, it's true that men are more likely to want to remain free to play the field. When you have two people with that mindset in a relationship, things can get sticky."

When asked if his opposition to gay marriage for personal reasons was hypocritical, Billings said that was "pure piffle."

"A lot of these people think we chose to be gay — which is like saying we chose to have blue eyes or brown hair — but they believe it," Billings said. "I'm as gay as Hulk Hogan wrapped in Paul Lynde, but I have no interest in marriage. I just know if I marry Arnold he'll let himself go and then I'll be stuck with the spitting image of Bookman from 'Good Times.' Sure, he'll scoff at his weight and say he's just big-boned, but I can already tell you that's a lie."

THE VASECTOMY

After the birth of our second child, my wife and I decided one of us should get fixed. Since she went to the trouble of birthing two kids, I figured I might as well be the one to go under the tin snips.

As the date of the event approached, a deep rot of nerves set in. I started to hit up my friends who'd gone through the same procedure for information. How bad did it hurt? After the procedure, did anything swell up to the size of an honorable mention-sized pumpkin? Was it easier to sing along to Journey afterwards? How bad did it hurt?

According to the guys I spoke to - who I've now determined are either much tougher than me or just filthy liars - it was no big deal. A fellow bandmate in Third Of Never (www.thirdofnever.com) had it done, and he told me all I had to do was relax and be still while on the table. I assured him that when that doctor started coming at my nards with the hammer and sickle that I wouldn't be working on a new jazzercise routine. Another guy told me he felt a slight pinch when he received the shot to numb the area, but other than that, it was no big deal.

The doctor could tell I was scared to death, so on our last visit before the blessed event, he wrote a prescription for something he promised would put my nerves at ease. Anybody that knows me will tell you I've never ingested anything stronger than a Pepsi, but at this particular juncture, I would have eaten a bowl of cocaine with crack gravy.

The day before the procedure, the tenants of the soon-to-be-reorganized area woke me up in the middle of the night for a chat.

"Dude, we understand the need for family planning, but we just want to make sure you've thought this thing through," said Bert.

"Yeah, you know, we've had some good times together, and we're worried that this procedure might cause some sort of disconnect," said Ernie.

"Fellas, first off, thanks for everything you've done for me over the years," I said. "Secondly, I've read all the articles and consulted with other guys who've gone through the procedure, and I've been told there's nothing to worry about."

"Really?" said Bert and Ernie in unison.

"Sure," I said. "You two are going to have to make room for a bag of frozen peas for a few days after the procedure, but other than that, it should be business as usual after a few weeks."

"OK, man, I guess you've done your research," said Ernie.

"Yeah, it would be a shame to put us out of business ... especially since you tricked that good-looking woman into marrying you," said Bert. "Kudos on that, by the way."

The next morning I lunged for those prescribed painkillers before my eyes had finished opening. To be sure I got the full effect, I took a straw and sucked every bit of pill residue out of the bottle. There seemed to be a hint of pill-related dust on the bottle cap, so I stuck it under my left arm pit.

Yes, I wanted to be sure I received the full painkilling power of those pills. Did I mention I was nervous about the procedure?

I then showered - which included preparing ground zero for the procedure. Without getting into to much detail here, let's just say I had to prepare for this procedure much the same way Yul Breynner prepared for "The King and I," only in a different time zone.

Since I was supposedly going to be high as a Georgia pine thanks to the doctor's prescription, my wife drove me to the doctor's office. We hadn't been on the road two minutes when we drove past a guy doing a little yard work. As if we'd driven into an old episode of "Three's Company," the guy was going down on some shrubbery with a massive set of hedge clippers. He looked like Edward Scissorhands after having consumed a gallon of Mountain Dew; lots of clippin', lots of snippin'.

By the time we arrived at the doctor's office, I was in the fetal position. As we made out way through the waiting room I realized that I was in deep trouble. Why was I in trouble? Because I was clear-headed and in full control of my faculties. My vision was perfect and all motor skills were working properly. All of this could only mean one thing: The painkillers were NOT WORKING.

I told a nurse that I needed something else for the pain, and she said what I'd already taken would be sufficient. After trying in vain to convince her the pharmacist had mistakenly replaced my proper medication with Folger's Crystals, I realized whatever was going to happen to me and my boys was going to happen while I was stone sober.

A few minutes later, my name was called and I realized it was time to be a man and do what I had to do. I took a deep breath, stood up and took a step towards the nurse and then several more steps in the other direction towards the parking lot. Just as I was about to reach the office door, the building went on lockdown and five male nurses tackled me in the lobby. I managed to fight off three of them, but the last two were former football players and they took me down.

Once I was in the chair/stirrup contraption, the doctor came in and seemed to think it was odd that I was sweating a river. He then had the nerve to ask what was wrong. I informed him that I wasn't used to making this amount of gravy in public, and he proceeded to ease my fears by ramming a needle up my transmission that felt like it had been sitting in molten lava overnight.

After they peeled me off the ceiling, the snipping and knotting began. To try and break the tension, I asked the doctor to tie that thing in a Windsor knot just to be sure. He then laughed so hard that he accidentally yanked on some wiring and my left ear flapped uncontrollably.

Whatever was in that needle must have worked because I didn't feel any of the snipping, burning, knotting - mainly because I was still hyperventilating from the shock of the light-pole-sized needle that pierced my flesh a few seconds before. Just as I'd started to calm down, Dr. Kervorkian's nephew plunged another 30-foot needle into a very sensitive area. By this time, I was speaking in a language that only mosquitoes could understand. My voice box was crowded by Bert and Ernie who were now trying to get away from the needles, scalpels and burning devices by pulling themselves ever further up into my body. Before it was over, I think they'd worked there way up around the middle of my chest.

With the procedure now over, I headed to the car. My wife got there a few hours before I did due to the fact that I was having to take iddy-biddy steps. Around the one-hour mark, I realized I was still several feet away from the car, so I tried to take a few normal-sized steps, which -- judging by the flash of nausea/vertigo that resulted -- was not a good idea.

Aside from the hundreds of potholes, the drive home was uneventful. Walking up the steps was a challenge, especially since the same bit of wiring the doctor accidentally yanked on was still causing my left ear to flap a little with every step. Once inside, I laid down and got extremely intimate with a bag of frozen peas.

I had the procedure done on a Friday with the intent of healing up over the weekend. While the constant application of frozen peas kept the swelling at bay, it didn't do much for the nausea that crept up every time I took a step. The first shower I took after being snipped was fun, especially since our shower could knock an elephant down at 20 paces. If you've never tried to take a shower with one hand positioned in a way to prevent the deluge of water from slamming into your nards, then I highly recommend it.

In time, everything worked out fine. My left ear stopped flapping every time I took a step and I was eventually able to get in and out of the shower in under three hours. I'm happy to say there were no major side effects - aside from the fact that whenever I hear Mike Krzyzewski's voice, my balls start to ache.

ABOUT THE AUTHOR

Five-time North Carolina Press Association award winner Jon Dawson writes humor and music columns for the Kinston Free Press. He lives on Earth with his smoking hot wife, two beautiful daughters, one dog and (as of this writing) two fish. Dawson is also a member of several bands, including Third Of Never, which features contributions from Who keyboardist John "Rabbit" Bundrick.

"Making Gravy In Public" is his first book.

For more information visit www.jondawson.com.

www.ingramcontent.com/pod-product-compliance
Lightning Source LLC
LaVergne TN
LVHW011157080426
835508LV00007B/449